CAN THE RED MAN HELP THE WHITE MAN?

A Denver Conference with the Indian Elders

edited by
SYLVESTER M. MOREY

GILBERT CHURCH, *Publisher*

New York

A LETTER FROM ROBERT L. BENNET

This document presents a great service to the American People, for it brings to their attention some of the basic life philosophy of American Indians. Its reading will create a better understanding of the reasons why Indian people not only have been able to cling to their basic philosophy but to resist the onslaught of counter-philosophies.

It is fortunate that at this time in history American Indian philosophy can contribute to the development of a proper perspective for changes in American society by proving a focus around which to build a better future.

Everyone owes a debt of gratitude to the Indian leadership and to the Myrin Institute, Inc., who formed a partnership to bring about the revelations contained in this document. I hope that the spirit which is engendered by this publication will permeate the thinking of everyone who has a concern about our society and that it will inspire them as it inspired me.

Robert L. Bennet
Commissioner of Indian Affairs

April 9, 1969

INTRODUCTION

In June, 1744, the Governor of the colony of Pennsylvania called a meeting in Lancaster of delegates from Pennsylvania, Maryland and Virginia, to meet with sachems of the Five Nations of the Iroquois Indians. For three weeks various problems were discussed. Then at the conclusion of the meeting on July 4, 1744, thirty-two years before the signing of the Declaration of Independence, the leading Iroquois chief, Canassatego, wound up his talk to the colonial delegates with this bit of sage advice to the white man: "We have one thing further to say, and that is We heartily recommend Union and a Good Agreement between you our Brethren. Never disagree, but preserve a strict Friendship for one another, and thereby you as well as we will become the Stronger. Our wise Forefathers established Union and Amity between the Five Nations; this has made us formidable. This has given us great weight and Authority with our Neighboring Nations. We are a Powerful confederacy, and by your observing the same Methods our wise Forefathers have taken, you will acquire fresh Strength and Power; therefore, whatever befalls you, never fall out with one another."

Few people today realize the true greatness of the American Indian and the magnitude of his intuitive wisdom; and as few realize the debt we owe the the the Indian, not only for the land in this country but for the ideas we have taken from him and brought into our way of life. For example, the inspiration behind the formation of the Federation of the Five Nations of the Iroquois, helped stimulate the union of our own thirteen colonies.

Long ago, Benjamin Franklin saw the Indian for what he was. He copied the League of the Five Nations in his Albany Plan of Union of 1754, and according to the Museum of the American Indian, our Constitution also incorporated some of its features.

Rudolf Steiner, the Austrian philosopher, said that much of the success of the white man in America was due to the intuitive ideas of the American Indian, ideas like those which inspired Benjamin Franklin, I'm sure. This line of thought caused me to become interested in Indian intuition.

Here is another example of how Indians have influenced our lives. The report of a lacrosse game between two tribes of the Iroquois in early days reads like the report of a big football game between two American colleges today. Before the event there were weeks of preparation and team practice. Then spectators traveled hundreds of miles to be present. Bets were handled by a betting master. The rival cheering sections lined up to cheer on opposite sides of the field. When the game was over, it was not so much the team that had won; it was the tribe.

From all I can find out, there were no organized team sports in Europe before the discovery of America. Stephan F. deBorhegyi, director of the Milwaukee Museum, writing on this point in 1960,* said that organized team sports in Europe prior to the 16th century seem to have been limited to tournaments and mock combats where no importance was attached to the team but all honor was given to the winning individuals. He says, "The New World idea of two teams engaged in competitive play was quite possibly an innovation to Europe." Today, in any event, we look on team sports in a way different from that of Europe. Here, when Yale plays Harvard in football, the triumph belongs not so much to the winning team as to the college. It is the victory of the tribe all over again. We have revived the Indian idea of tribes and their teams. Even our TV broadcasters refer to college football games as "tribal rites."

I was still keenly interested in the whole story of our American Indian when, in 1967, I discovered that the Commissioner of Indian Affairs, Robert L. Bennett, was a full-blooded Oneida, one of the tribes of the famous Five Nations of the Iroquois. It was then that a series of meetings was set up that culminated in the Conference of Indian Elders held in Denver in 1968, as reported in this publication.

The Commissioner was good enough to select the Indians who took part in the conference, and at his bidding, Arrow,

*America's Ball Game, by Stephan F. deBorhegyi, Natural History Magazine, January, 1960

Inc., a non-profit organization devoted entirely to helping in Indian affairs, undertook the task of making all the arrangements. The Myrin Institute sponsored the project.

The points which came up at this meeting concerning the Indian's and the white man's views of proper education are not new. As long ago as 1744, the same Canassatego just mentioned surprised the colonists in this respect. In June of that year the Governor of the colony of Pennsylvania with representatives from Maryland and Virginia opened their meeting with the Iroquois sachems by offering to send eight or ten young Indians, selected by the Five Nations, to Williamsburg, and there to give them a good education. Canassatego rose to speak for the Indians. He said that Indians had already had experience with white man's schools and that their young men had returned to their tribes neither white men nor Indians. He said that if the whites would select a dozen or two of their boys, the Indians would send them to Onondaga, where the great council of the Iroquois would take care of their education and bring them up in what was the best manner to make men of them.

So you see that since colonial times Indians have felt that there is something missing in the white man's idea of education. What is missing is the Indian's intuitive feeling, as contrasted with our intellectual curiosity, about nature and life. The Indian approaches life through his heart. White men would never say that the animals are their brothers, the earth is their mother, or that the beans, the corn and the squash are the three sisters. But the Indian says it and means it.

Think for a moment of the Indians' way of naming things, in contrast to our way. One senses how open the true Indian has always been to what he sees, and how we, on the other hand, inject our own feelings, our personal likes and dislikes, into our view of the external world and, therefore, fail to see beings and things as they actually are.

I come from a little town near Saratoga Springs, New York. At Saratoga, in the old days, there was a small Mohawk village. The name, Saratoga, means in Mohawk, "the place where ashes float." That is how the Indians viewed the springs where alkaline or mineral bubbles float. The name Niagara refers to the river below the falls, where it narrows into a throat or neck to split the land in two. The name means "gorge throat." The moose was "he who eats off trees"; raccoon was "he who tears with his hands." The Indian saw objects and beings without sentiment or personal feeling, and labeled them for what they were — or for what they appeared to him to be. Men were named in the same way. Red Jacket, a famous Seneca orator, was raised up as merit chief in his tribe, and then, according to custom, was given a new name. He was called "Keeper Awake" because of his great power of oratory. The chief who gave American arms the worst military defeat we suffered at the hands of the Indians was a quiet little man, noted for keeping his own counsel. The Indians named him "Little Turtle." Indian names in those early days fitted a man, because the Indian saw into the man's nature and named him for what he was.

It is interesting to compare these names with the names Europeans gave to Indian corn — in the days after the discovery of America. When our corn was first taken back to Europe, the European considered it an outlandish, coarse and weird kind of grain. For this reason, and also because no one was quite sure where America was, many strange names were given to it. Some thought it came from Asia. Also, in those days, Continental Europeans regarded the Turks who were Asiatics and who had then conquered Europe all the way to the Adriatic, as rough, uncultured enemies. To express contempt for a thing, it was common to call it Turkish. And that was their feeling for this coarse, overgrown grain that came from the New World. So it was called "Turkish Corn." The name stemmed from the feelings of the Europeans and had nothing to do with the vegetable itself. In England, at that time, the matter was solved even more simply. There were differences between the English and the Welsh. The Welsh were considered rough and uncultured and so our corn was labeled "Welsh Corn."

In becoming civilized, scientific and intellectual, we have

become increasingly aware of ourselves. But to see the world as it really is, we must, at times, be able to forget ourselves, our desires, our prejudices, even our science and our intellectual knowledge. Then the world of inspiration and intuition can speak to us directly, as it spoke to the Indian and to the ancient Greek and Hebrew.

The Indian way of life — the Indian manner of thinking and observing the world — is different from the white man's way. It is enormously important for white men, especially teachers and those who have to do with educating our youth, to understand this. If our youth could see this difference — and broaden themselves to the point where they could master intellectuality, like the white man, and still develop intuitively, like the Indian - they would bring balance and harmony into their own lives and the lives of those around them.

Young people are on the rampage today because they sense that something is missing from life. They don't know what it is, and neither do those around them seem to know. What they lack is something inner — something to do with the heart and with a true understanding of the meaning of life.

Years ago an old Pueblo Indian spoke to Carl Jung, the famous psychologist. The few words of the old Indian, if understood, offer the solution to today's problem with youth. He said that white men were mad, crazy. White men believe you think with your head, but every Indian knows you think with your heart.

The point is that Indians do think with their hearts. But also it is true that white men think with their brains. A complete man does both.

I believe this old Indian's statement sums up the attitude of the American Indian even today, as exemplified by this Denver Conference of Indian Elders. It also expresses what the Myrin Institute hopes will be inspired by the conference and the publication of this report.

* * * * * * * *

The week-long conference reported here was held in Denver, Colorado in June 1968. It was sponsored by the Myrin Institute of New York City, a non-profit Foundation organized to promote adult education, and it was arranged through the cooperation of Robert L. Bennett, then United States Commissioner of Indian Affairs, and Mr. E. Thomas Colosimo, Executive Secretary of Arrow, Inc., a non-profit organization dealing exclusively with projects aimed to help American Indians.

Representing the Myrin Institute were Dr. Franz E. Winkler, President of the Institute, and Sylvester M. Morey, Chairman.

Mr. E. Thomas Colosimo attended as representative of Arrow, Inc.

The meetings were chaired by Mr. Allen Quetone (Kiowa); Mr. Will Rogers, Jr., (Cherokee), Assistant Commissioner of Indian Affairs, opened the first meeting.

Others participating in the conference were:

Ben Black Elk, an Oglala Sioux from Manderson, S.D.;
David Kindle, A Navajo from Shiprock, N.M.;
Alfred Bowman, a Navajo from Shiprock, N.M.;
Guy Quetone, a Kiowa from Carnegie, Okla.;
Alex Saluskin, a Yakima from Toppenish, Wash.;
Chief Joshua Wetsit, an Assiniboine from Wolf Point, Montana.

Mr. Clarence Wesley (San Carlos Apache), Mr. Francis McKinley (Ute), Mr. Sydney Carney (Seneca) and Mr. Forrest Gerard (Blackfeet) were also present for some of the sessions.

Sylvester M. Morey

CONTENTS

CHAPTER I

THE CONFERENCE STARTS

The Conference with the Indian Elders started on a Sunday afternoon in late June 1968. The gentlemen from the Myrin Institute, Dr. Winkler and Mr. Morey, came in by plane from New York just after lunch. They found Mr. E. Thomas Colosimo, Executive Director of Arrow, Inc., already there. Arrow, Inc. a non-profit organization dedicated to helping American Indians had made all the physical arrangements for the meeting. Originally there had been hopes that the conference could be arranged in a country setting where the discussion could take place under trees in an atmosphere more in tune with the Indian way of life. But the Hyatt House in the center of Denver had been finally picked, as it seemed to work out best for all concerned.

Mr. Colosimo reported that Mr. Will Rogers, Jr. (Cherokee), Assistant to the Commissioner of Indian Affairs, Robert L. Bennett, was there, and an introductory session was to start immediately. Mr. Rogers presided during the first meeting, which was largely a "get acquainted" affair.

In addition to the gentlemen already mentioned, there were present Mr. Allen Quetone (Kiowa) permanent chairman of the conference, Mr. David Kindle and Mr. Alfred Bowman (Navajo), Mr. Alexander Saluskin (Yakima) Chief Joshua Wetsit (Assiniboine) and Mr. Clarency Wesley (San Carlos Apache).

1

Mr. Guy Quetone (Kiowa), father of Allen Quetone, was held up in Fort Worth, Texas, by a delayed airliner, and Mr. Ben Black Elk (Oglala Sioux) was also detained and did not appear for the Sunday meeting. Mr. Forrest Gerard (Blackfeet), Mr. Francis McKinley (Ute) and Mr. Sidney Carney (Seneca) came later in the week. At the start Mr. Morey told in some detail of his special interest in Indians and what his studies had disclosed.

Some years ago Mr. Morey had discovered that the native wisdom of American Indians had made substantial contributions to American culture. As a result, he spent several years doing research on the Indians of Colonial days, presenting his findings in PROCEEDINGS published by the Myrin Institute in 1961. This paper had the special purpose of pointing out specific Indian culture traits which affected the white men who came later to America.

Dr. Winkler had felt that there might still be much intuitive wisdom among American Indians, especially the Indian elders, which could be put to use in overcoming some of the youth problems of today. At Dr. Winkler's suggestion Mr. Morey had proposed this meeting to the Honorable Robert Bennett, who was then Commissioner of Indian Affairs in Washington, and himself an Oneida Indian. Mr. Bennett thought well of the project and arranged to invite those present to the meeting.

At first, the Indian Elders were reluctant to speak on the subject of how Indian tradition and moral training might be of help to white people. They were self-conscious because there were so many problems with their own young people. True, they may have been reserved because of the desire to see whether those who called the conference had something truly worthwhile in mind. Dr. Winkler assured them, however, that white people were having the same difficulties as they with alcohol, drugs, crime and unrest all over the nation. These were common problems. And he convinced them of the serious intent to see whether and how the discussion of Indian tribal customs, legends, ceremonies, festivals, and tribal views of how to instruct youth could shed fresh light on the subject of developing morality and wisdom in the common culture.

Detailed discussion on these points was put off until the Monday session. At that time the two secretaries were to have tape recorders in readiness. The secretaries for the meetings were Mrs. Dene Curtis, a Cherokee, and Miss Linda Bernal, a Taos. Miss Bernal is the niece of the Governor of the Taos Indians of New Mexico. The governor had planned to be at the meeting but had to send his regrets at the last minute due to tribal affairs. He extended a warm invitation to those present to come to Taos after the Denver meeting. Unfortunately, this was not possible to arrange.

Mr. Allen Quetone explained to Dr. Winkler and Mr. Morey how Indian conferences were conducted. He said that each Indian would be given a chance to express his opinion and to say whatever he wanted to say on each topic under discussion. In accordance with Indian custom, no one would interrupt when another had the floor. Also, it was expected that all would give full attention when others spoke.

Mr. Morey said that he was delighted to hear this, as reports of Indian meetings in Colonial days stated that the proceedings were exactly as Mr. Quetone had outlined them. The English and French in those days were deeply impressed by the Indian councils: by the gravity of the proceedings and the attention given by each participant. The Jesuit priest Lafitau who lived with the Iroquois around 1650 compared an Iroquois tribal council with the Roman Senate in the early days of the Roman Republic.

After the first meeting was adjourned, discussion continued at dinner that night at the Brown Palace Hotel. In fact, discussions continued all week, not only at formal sessions in the morning and afternoon but also at lunch and often at breakfast and dinner as well. There was much to tell and much to learn.

The first regular sessions opened promptly Monday morning. The meetings were held on the top floor of the Hyatt House in rooms set aside for the week.

Mr. Allen Quetone (Kiowa), permanent chairman, called the meeting to order. He is a handsome, husky man about 5 feet 10

3

inches in his early forties, a former student at the University of Oklahoma, a graduate of Oklahoma City University with a degree in business administration, now superintendant of Indian reservations in Horton, Kansas for the Bureau of Indian Affairs. He served two terms as Vice-President of the National Congress of American Indians, was first Chairman of the Tribal Council of twenty-three tribes, and has been extremely active in many other tribal and educational organizations. As chairman of the Denver meeting, he showed marked skill in bringing out interesting discussions.

On the pages that follow are selections from the taped statements of the Indian Elders and comments by Dr. Winkler and others attending the Denver meeting.

It will be noted that a speaker did not always follow the topic discussed by the previous speaker. This was because the Indian participants were asked, before they came to Denver, to be ready to tell about the history, legends, rituals etc. of their own people. Therefore, in some sessions there was no attempt to hold to a topic or topics. Instead, at such times the meetings were more like story telling affairs with each man free to say what he had on his mind.

ALLEN QUETONE, Moderator: This is a joint project sponsored by Arrow, Inc., Myrin Institute and the Bureau of Indian Affairs to record your discussions on Indian traditions, rituals, legends and other cultural values.

The purpose is to determine to what extent the old wisdoms, philosophies and intuition of the Indian could be utilized to help solve the complex social ills of the present. We will try to cover that part of Indian life that is important to the success of this project as envisioned by Mr. Morey and Dr. Winkler, with emphasis on education, morality and character, man's relation to nature, man's relation to man, which will include Indian ceremonials, legends, the Indian way of life and religion. This is an opportunity to state what you would like to see perpetuated, those things in the Indian

4

way of life that each of you would like to see taught today to young people.

This first-day meeting is primarily to discuss the purposes of this project and some of the things that you will be asked to talk about and the methods we will use in recording each of your statements.

Dr. Winkler will first present his views and ideas on the subject matter to be discussed.

DR. FRANZ WINKLER: Mr. Morey and I have had for years many interests in common, among them a sincere admiration for the spirit of the American Indian people. The occasion of meeting such distinguished members of these people is, therefore, a very special privilege for us; a privilege made even greater by your agreement to discuss with us some of the most urgent problems of our time.

Until Mr. Morey took the initiative for this conference, neither he nor I had had any contact with official or private organizations concerned with Indian affairs. Thus, we are only superficially informed on the many projects intended to improve the relationship between white and red America. Yet we hope that just because we are outsiders, we may have some new views to offer that could be of help to this all-important goal.

My own affection for the American Indian stems from my childhood days when Karl May's *Winnetou** stirred an undying enthusiasm in the hearts of many young Middle Europeans. However, there is also a more objective cause for my participation in this conference, a cause that may be related to the basic tenets of my profession. It is the physician's natural concern with the problem of healing, not only with regard to the individual but also to society as a whole. This concern has led me to a study of history and a

*Karl Friedrich May, 1842-1912, the "German J. Fenimore Cooper." His seventy books have sold over fifteen million copies in German editions alone, and have been translated into more than twenty languages, but not English. Long after he had written his masterpieces about the American West he made his first trip to America, at the age of sixty-six.

search for the underlying causes for the rise and fall of civilizations. There are two factors which seem to be decisive for the health of a civilization: one is the kind of relationship the invader maintains with the best of native culture, and the other is the care he gives to the prótection of the country's natural beauty and resources.

History never stands still. Ancient cultures tend to become static and thus need at times the influx of fresh blood and of new impulses to stimulate further growth. But civilizations imposed even by the most powerful invaders are bound to fail unless the newcomers are willing and able to graft their own ideas on existing cultures. There are several examples of such successful grafting in the history of the Old World, as for instance in Russia or China, where a succession of nationally and racially foreign conquerors rejuvenated, rather than destroyed, native civilizations.

A country is more than the sum total of its material resources. It is a living entity that must be treated with respect and love if it is to give true happiness and health to the people making their home in it. In this country, the Indians represent unquestionably a true manifestation of the grandiose and stark natural beauty that once distinguished the expanses of the American continent. The tragic mistake of the white conquerors was to suppress, rather than sublimate, the living forces inherent in the conquered land. Originating in an entirely different environment, they never learned to sink their roots into the soil of the New World.

The tree of Indian civilization had deep and healthy roots, but it failed to send its trunk upward at the rapid pace necessitated by the growing world population and the increasing demands for material goods. Thus, the far more materialistically minded Europeans might have indeed supplied the necessary modernizing impulse to the ancient, but somewhat immobile, genius of Indian tribal society.

If a tree possessing healthy roots grows too slowly, or does not bear enough fruit to fill the demands of a new era, a grafting implantation of fast growing and highly productive life forms may perfect the organism. If, however, the roots are separated from the crown, the roots must wither for lack of light and air, while the crown will be cut off from the sap rising from the soil. Thus the Indian who has provided the root for the culture of this continent has suffered—prevented from direct participation in the task of building a new nation. White America, on the other hand, while branching out rapidly in material enterprise, is no longer nourished by the basic spiritual resources without which a nation cannot retain its health.

It is more than symbolic that the white man's failure to establish a close relationship with the native civilization is reflected in his tragic disregard for the integrity and beauty of the land he has conquered. Every year vast areas, once alive with irreplaceable beauty and adorned with natural wealth, are buried under concrete and steel, as if the tree of a growing culture could survive cut off from its roots in the living soil.

ALLEN QUETONE: Mr. Morey is a businessman and Dr. Winkler is a medical doctor. They have some ideas and interests in the Indian area, and as Dr. Winkler just said, he and Mr. Morey believe that the Indian culture, the Indian way of life, has influenced some of the institutions of this country. The poorness of health he refers to is the way our country is going today, losing some of the finer things of life, the way of life that is good. He feels that unless something is done to stabilize or get the country back in balance, this country will go down as a lot of others have in the past. They feel that Indian values and Indian ways have many more good things to contribute to the present society in which we live, the white man's world.

Because of the relatively recent history that the Indian has experienced, there is a tendency to look at the white man's world with a futility, a hopelessness as to any thought of trying to perpetuate or retain the Indian life. Each of you

7

men in your own areas know of Indian people who are making an attempt to keep their Indian way, although even within their own tribe there is a division as to the traditional way and the modern thought or direction. All tribes have traditional groups, conservative groups, and these are the ones that perpetuate some of the traditional Indian ways.

In this discussion there are two areas we wish to cover: the tribal way as well as individual experience. Of course, information as to personal experience will differ somewhat from what the tribal way is, and especially the tribal way as it might apply to present day life.

We can start around the table, to see what ideas or suggestions you may have on the purposes of this project. Will you begin Mr. Bowman?

ALFRED BOWMAN: In educating our young people, the Indian family is better qualified to teach their young at home or acquire somebody who has the knowledge of the legends and stories that could do it at home. What they are learning through the schools, these are secondary efforts. It is not the family way of teaching their youngsters.

If they want to teach their Indian culture, they should be encouraged to do that. If they are educated up to where they merged into the other culture, that is all right too. It is better that they should have the choice. The Navajos haven't really fully adopted the white man's culture. I have worked with my own people for the last thirty-three years, and not at any time did they say they envy the white people how they lived. It is just a removed thing to them.

The trouble is, they weren't encouraged to follow their own culture and traditions. They are kind of victims of the circumstances. They should be encouraged to practice their own culture in their own homes.

ALLEN QUETONE: In other words, the Navajos still have many of their Indian ways.

ALFRED BOWMAN: White man dances are just a social gathering, but our dances are ceremonial, and the Indian healing dances should be divorced from the regular shows. This gives a bad impression.

There is only one dance in the Navajo culture, called the Squaw Dance, where the girls dance with the men. It is a healing ceremonial dance. But since the young people have done the white man's dances, they like to keep on without end.

DAVID KINDLE:* I like to say thanks to the Chairman, to Dr. Winkler and these representatives that came from all parts of the country to consult on these vital questions.

Our Apache friend this morning told about their ceremony where the girl came into womanhood.** I still think our youth should go through those processes of ceremony.

In Navajo custom, a man erects a dwelling place, a hogan. The head of the home comes over and blesses the home first. He uses the corn pollen, dedicated to the east, south, west and north, then within the interior of the home, that the home will be well established and the inhabitants who occupy that home will be blessed from the Higher Spirit and everything will be all well. That's the way he does it before he moves into his new home.

If they want to make a ceremony, he has to have a man that knows the ceremony to be brought in. They start a chant, the home blessing, which has twelve verses. Then they dedicate it on four sides like before, and he makes a prayer offering that all the inhabitants of the particular home, the people in the neighborhood, also the chiefs and those in authority, would be benefited from the Higher Spirit. That is the way the prayer runs. Everything would be all right to the inhabitants and the people that surround this area.

Most of the ceremonies and chants are to have blessings upon the people that inhabit the land there. The Yib-be-chai ceremony is a nine-day ceremony for the healing of the patient. Another dance, a three-night ceremony, called Corral

---

*Mr. Kindle spoke in Navajo. Alfred Bowman interpreted.
**This discussion begins on page 125.

Dance or Fire Dance, is a healing ceremony, too. It is true, it is a dance, but the dance is applying for blessing from the Higher Spirit.

These three major dances of the Navajo Tribe are healing ceremonies for the patients, the prayers are offered for all the people gathered there. People come from the east, from the south, from the west, from the north, with one accord—they are to receive blessings and goodwill. That is why they dress for these gatherings; nice moccasins, nice buckskin leggings, turquoise belt, beads, because it is done reverently. They have to be dressed in their best to attend these ceremonies, because prayers are offered for all that come.

We have a very high respect for these ceremonies, especially the older people in my age group. The younger generation that went to the white man's school, they come down and try to make it a social affair. It is a ceremony, not a social gathering, and those in my age group still revere these ceremonies.

Our prayers in all these ceremonies run this way: Our Mother Earth will be blessed with all the fruit she can produce, to provide food for all the inhabitants. We pray that the sun, everything, will be well and blessing may be bestowed upon the nation, all the people that live with us and around, our neighbors and the animal kingdom. That's the way our prayer runs.

ALLEN QUETONE: Might Mr. Kindle comment on why the prayer is for everybody?

DAVID KINDLE: The origin is that we all live on this Mother Earth. We have an equal share, irrespective of where we are on this earth. We get whatever comes from the sun and it would be a selfish way of doing to keep it for oneself. That's why we spread it out for everybody.

ALEX SALUSKIN: The gentlemen from the Navaho country touched on the basic Indian culture as the way our old people lived. That culture is the same as ours in the Northwest, especially the Yakima people. Our culture in the plateau country is similar to that of the plains.

10

Our people had an Indian religion which was known as the Pom Pom religion. This was handed down from some of the men and women who had come alive again after being dead for one or two days. From that it became a law for the Indians never to bury the deceased unless he had laid in state for three whole days. The Creator may send him back with a message for the survival of the Indian people, a teaching as to what is the right way to live.

These people through their religion had a Sabbath day, and on the fifth day you commenced to clean yourself. On the sixth day you stopped labor, and on the Sabbath day you worshipped. This Pom Pom religion was singing in prayer-like songs (the white people call it chanting) and a religious dance, once around the holy land which was marked out in the center of the long house, to the rhythm of seven drums which were beat in unison. Out of this, the teachings were handed down to the young people.

Those songs as handed down from deceased parents, uncles or sisters through a dream—they woke up with an enlightenment and they immediately commenced singing these religious songs—were teaching as to how they should carry on from there.

When a youngster, I was taught by some of these well-trained people that understood Indian religion. It was not a parent that was undertaking the teaching of the young boy or girl, it was an elder related either to grandpa or grandma. They became the tutors. The children were taken from their parents after they became about six-seven-eight, up to thirteen years old. They were sent out for a spirit quest. They looked for the power in the wilderness and fasted for a minimum of three days and nights and a maximum of five days and nights. During the hardship, fighting for survival out in the wilderness, without anything to eat, no tools to gain energy, competing with wild animals and dark cold nights, the little fellows got down and prayed, asked the Great Spirit to help them to survive the ordeal. During the course, some of these people were blessed and

11

they carried the blessing on and handed it down to their children, and also later on they would become tutors to teach the same things that the Indian must follow.

Now we come to manhood and womanhood. The young maiden was watched and supervised very closely by her parents or an elder who was the tutor of that young lady. When the time came, the parents of another noted family who had a young man coming into manhood, would have a desire to acquire this young lady, who was already trained to do woman's work, for their son's mate. To propose, they sent a noted man of the highest integrity to make the proposition and, of course, the young woman's family also expected that at the end they were going to realize something for their daughter. They were proud people, so if they accepted something of little value, then their proper station in the society wouldn't be recognized. Therefore they asked as much as they could get for their daughter.

In the marriage ceremony the young bride and groom were brought before their families and relatives. These would place down certain valuables for them to sit on. Once they sat on that prepared seat, came the second part of the ceremony. The valuable bead work from the bride's side was bestowed upon them by placing it on the bride. On the other hand, the men from the groom's side cast their blessing to their relatives with their heirlooms. Each time that the young lady had goods put on her shoulders, the relatives from the man's family would take them and walk off with them and acknowledge them by expressing well wishes to the bride. When the man's garment, or whatever gift, was placed on the young man, the bride's family would come and pick that up and acknowledge it in the same way. The ceremony would go until these goods were exhausted. Each family showed how well-to-do it was by presenting such gifts in honor of the marriage.

This conclusion of the marriage ceremony made it binding that at no time would the young man abandon his wife. He was pledged under their law and custom.

If I can go back to my own childhood experience (I must have been about seven years old), we stopped by a great big lake there to catch some fish for supplies to go up to Huckleberry Mountain. An eagle had been killed. There was an old medicine man with us, besides my grandfather. He said, "Well, Alexander, you're going to have to take that bird back up to that butte where they killed him." (Big Jacket Mountain was about three-four miles away.) I thought they were kidding, when my dad said, "The quicker you get away at it, Alexander, the better for you. If you get up in the higher altitude, you're going to get away from the darkness. In the timber it will get dark and you'll get lost. You wouldn't reach that point." So they handed me a little bowie knife and one of those Indian canes they used to use. The bird was almost as big as I was. They tied him on my back and very reluctantly I started to walk.

I walked through tall fern and brush about as high as myself. I was wondering if I could make a howl like I was attacked and maybe they would feel sorry for me, come looking for me and ask me to come back. I let out a lusty howl like I was attacked by some beast and I could hear my echo all around those hills and across the lake. I really got frightened and thought, "It won't be long before the wild beasts hear me and come looking for me. They will devour me and I will get killed." So, from there on, I traveled as hard as I could until I was almost out of wind. I got out of that dense forest, up to the highest peak, and the sun went down. I didn't want to go back through that timber. I thought I was safer out there with that bird. At the same time I was angry at that bird, so I laid him down quite a ways away from me. Next to a big boulder where there was considerable pine needles, I lay down to take a rest. The next morning when I woke up, I was lying right next to that big bird.

I can't tell you what experiences I had during that night. Seems like I had slept all night until my father got worried about me because I didn't come back. He tracked me right up to where I was lying. They didn't leave me there like the teaching we used to have when there weren't any white people. They had to leave them three nights and days at least. They were given the guiding spirit, as we call it, the power.

JOSHUA WETSIT: I did not have much schooling but I study in my own way, study my Indian language and study English and that's what made me a leader for the last fifty years. I worked on a farm most of the time to make my living. At the same time, a good many of my people are worse off than I am. They don't have any schooling. Those that had schooling didn't stay on the reservation, so that left me with many people to help.

This Indian education, I know little about it. I was born in 1886. I could remember very distinctly since I was four years old about how our people change after the white man came. I see the tribe going along; the children walking, some are riding, some are playing. They only make maybe two-three miles' journey, stop there, keep moving and doing their hunting, trying to make a living. Eventually we get a little more equipment, settle down for gardens and make our living that way, the white man's way.

My great-grandfather in 1832 was called to Washington during Andrew Jackson's time. My great-grandfather was a great fighter in those days, so he wore porcupine quills and fringes. He had hairs for fringes because he killed a lot of enemies. The ermine skin he used for war shirts showed he was the highly honored; the horned headdress with a long trailer of tail feathers. There were no treaty negotiations. He, his wife, another man and his wife, went and stayed two winters and came back. The President was very much pleased with them. They were taken up to see New York City.

After he came back, he told the people what he had seen. They accused him, "You stay too long. You must've sell us out. We didn't authorize you to. This is our land, our property that's holy, that is not to sell." Inside of two years, they assassinated him because they thought he went crazy. It's his brother, my great-uncle, First to Fly, whose name was given to me when I was made chief twenty-five years ago.

This land, we appreciate that. When the eye of the Great Spirit rises in the morning, we stand and worship and thank Him for that wonderful land that we're living in. Anything that's pretty we use to pray with, because the Great Spirit made that. That's the way our people trained us. They tell stories, Indian stories, they wind up into meaning something of what we see on earth. The Great Spirit does that. So therefore I say now that the religion is the holy thing, to love one another. Love and kindness, those are the main laws we have.

GUY QUETONE: Today we're together almost on the same ground. We have drifted back to the place of beginning. We are at daggers with each kind of race, according to history today.

It was that way at the beginning. We first got acquainted. It could be a white man or some other race, but first of all we kind of met on the same ground, as the animal spirit. Were you ever on a farm and a passerby came down the road? You had a dog and his dog was coming behind his wagon. Instead of a welcome, the first thing one does is jump at the other and try to choke his throat out. They mix up there for a while and either they make friends or one runs away. That's the way we meet—as equal groups first; not knowing each other, we go to the throats. Either one of us takes flight and runs off, or we make friends.

What is being brought out here today is one of the greatest things that could happen to our world. It only brings the truth about life in the beginning of races and how they felt towards each other and how they lived since discovery of America and different tribes. I am happy to be here to associate with my fellow man.

BEN BLACK ELK: I'm Ben Black Elk, son of Black Elk. I'm seventy years old now. I had four long braids when I went to

15

school. I lost my mother when I was a year old and my sister raised me.

I didn't learn from books. I learned from my people, the old folks, and my father was my best teacher in my life. There are three books out that concern my father. One is *Black Elk Speaks.*

To start off, as Indians, money doesn't mean anything to us. If you give the needy more, you're a man. Today as we progress along, I feel that we've lost a lot of the heritage of our Indians, the spiritual life of the Indians. Around the campfire, our history is written on the four corners of the earth, the winds, to be captured by Indian wise men and then to be handed down generation to generation around campfires. We know that we are the people of knowledge. We present our knowledge to our children to carry it on.

CHAPTER II

INDIAN BELIEFS

At yesterday's meeting Chief Joshua Wetsit told the group
that he had received his Indian name "Chief First to Fly" from
his great-uncle when he was made chief twenty-five years ago.
He omitted saying that he had arrived in Denver with his car
and trailer, his title prominently displayed on the trailer. This
had created a little excitement of its own in the parking lot at
the Denver motel.

One wonders about that title "First to Fly" which the Chief
got from his great-uncle. Was the great-uncle the first to fly in a
plane, or has it a spiritual significance? The Chief's
great-grandfather visited Andrew Jackson in 1832. This makes
one wonder how long ago the great-uncle lived. Too bad the
question was not raised and answered in Denver.

The Chief had also brought his wife Sarah Martin Wetsit, and
with her a woman companion from the Assiniboine tribe. The
ladies came to the luncheon Monday and found the discussions
so interesting that they stayed for the afternoon meetings. They
keenly followed all that was said but, Indian style, they
remained in the background and listened. Two other interested
Indian women were the young secretaries, Mrs. Curtis and Miss
Bernal. When away from the meeting room they talked with
animation about what they had heard and on their own added
their opinions and much interesting information about their
own people.

At the start of the first meeting Dr. Winkler referred to his
childhood days when he read Karl May's *Winnetou* as a young
Middle European. Dr. Winkler was born in Austria, obtained his
medical degree at the University of Vienna. He came to this
country about thirty years ago and has practiced medicine in
New York City since 1941. He teaches at the New York Medical
College, is President of the Myrin Institute. He acts as medical

17

adviser to several schools, is a trustee of Adelphi University and is author of the book, *Man: The Bridge Between Two Worlds.**

The real work of the conference started at yesterday's session. Before going on to the conversations of the second day it will be helpful to dwell for a moment upon the trend of the discussion during the first day.

When Dr. Winkler led off the first session with the key point that, as a physician, he came to this meeting as one interested in healing, not only the individual but society as a whole, it became apparent that the Indians were quite prepared to speak on this subject. All spoke about their religion and how it serves to bring blessings and healing through their dances, ceremonies and rituals. Alfred Bowman made a special point of the fact that Indian dances are not for social purposes, but for healing. Alexander Saluskin, among other things, spoke of the spirit quest of the Indian, which is, or was, the great Indian way of finding his path in life: healing from a physical as well as from a spiritual point of view.

David Kindle spoke of the Navajo's prayer to the Higher Spirit for all the people "that live with us and around, our neighbors and the animal kingdom." Joshua Wetsit said "this land, we appreciate that. When the eye of the Great Spirit rises in the morning, we stand and worship and thank Him for this wonderful land we're living in."

Dr. Winkler had already stressed the tragic mistake of white conquerors who have suppressed rather than sublimated the living forces in a conquered land. In America, he pointed out, the white man's failure to establish a close relationship with the native civilization is reflected in his tragic disregard for the integrity and beauty of the land he has conquered.

The brief statements of the Indian elders, even on this first day, revealed much about their culture—a culture that has a strong connection with the soil of America and its animal and

*Originally published by Harper & Row. A new edition is available from Gilbert Church, Inc., 475 Fifth Avenue, New York, N.Y. 10017.

18

plant nature. White Americans have never understood or wanted to understand this primordial basis for their civilization, much less considered the consequences of ignoring and suppressing it.

And now let us move to the meeting room for the next session.

ALLEN QUETONE: To begin this second day, Dr. Winkler would like to comment on the remarks made yesterday, as well as on today's topic.

DR. FRANZ WINKLER: From the remarks made, especially during our less formal discussions, I gather that you are just as worried about the attitude of your children as any comparable group of white people is today about its own. In other words, the red and the white man have an urgent problem in common that ought to make them even more aware of how desperately they need each other's understanding and cooperation.

First I should like to say a few words about the problems of young people in the white community, problems which in my medical as well as consulting practice I have to face almost daily. The depth of the emotional crises afflicting white youth today is clearly shown in the wide use of mind-changing drugs. Scientists and experts in this field seem still at a loss to find the cause for the drug addiction, rebellion and suicidal tendencies among young people, but a family physician, if he has their confidence, learns of a very simple explanation. This explanation, expressed by the young people themselves, although often in vague terms, can be summarized thus: "Life as it is, is not worth living. It promises neither adventure nor deeper meaning, and so it can be endured only by escaping into a dream world."

In other words, the dreary, materialistic civilization of the white man fails to offer the spiritual motivation young people need if they are to face life joyfully and master it. It is certainly not a coincidence that some rather effective methods of saving a youth's emotional health have been found in Indian-type "wilderness survival courses" which permit young people to draw strength from nature, while improving their physical and emotional stamina. That such courses do not suffice to solve the problems of youth is partly due to the fact that the underlying *spiritual* principles of this kind of upbringing, once well known to the Indian, are no longer understood. Nature can be the great healer of man only if her gifts are accepted in the reverential mood of the old Indian way, the mood of gratitude and respect for her as the living manifestation of the Great Spirit.

White youth, deprived of spiritual motivation, suffers from a lack of inner resources. Indian youth suffers from a denial of the *material* opportunities in which every citizen of an affluent country ought to share. One would therefore expect that all intelligent and active Indians would long to participate in the philosophy and the ways of white civilization. That this is not the case can be explained only by the red man's instinctive knowledge that materialistic achievements alone will never bring happiness to the heart of an Indian. Thus, Indian youth lives in a limbo between two worlds. One of these worlds is represented by tribal life and the beauty of ancient ways and customs. But this world offers no share in the wealth of technological civilization and it has grown almost incomprehensible to a generation no longer brought up in the old way. The other world promises material goods and outer success but with inner emptiness. Thus, in despair, Indian youths, as well as their white brothers and sisters, only too often seek refuge in a shadow world of alcohol and drugs that are honorable in neither the one world nor the other.

The solution to this problem is not easy, but I should like to offer a few suggestions. Do not nurture in your children a sense of bitterness and vengefulness against the white people, for those who have committed the real crimes against the Indians have long since gone from this earth. No matter of what race he is, or of what nation, no one can be held responsible for the sins of his forefathers. Moreover, if my understanding of the true Indian of old is correct, I think he would have blamed himself for a defeat, rather than his enemy. Long before the white man came to this land, something must have happened to the Indians to make them vulnerable to defeat.

I also believe that racism is basically foreign to Indian thinking, as shown by the willingness of many tribes to adopt children of other races into their community. Thus I hope that equality and equal opportunity for the Indians will never be sought by raising the question of race.

On the other hand, I do not recommend for Indian youth docile acceptance of the white man's materialistic attitude and pitifully one-sided education. My suggestion, therefore, is—and I know that I simply repeat what others must have said many times before—that the wisest among traditionally-minded Indians form councils to be responsible for the upbringing of their own children. Such upbringing could kindle in the still open hearts of the young a sense of wonder and adventure. Native schools might be located near State forests or wilderness areas, for without access to undisturbed nature, education can never fulfill its true mission. Naturally an intense physical training would have to go hand in hand with the training of mind and heart, so that the Indians would regain their lost pride, not only in their culture, but also in their physical strength.

Only the red men themselves, in my opinion, can rightly train their own children in accordance with the needs of their physical and spiritual nature. But once the foundation has been laid, the white man's intellectual and technological education should be added. Young Indians, their hearts and bodies trained in the Indian way and their minds prepared to tackle the challenges of our scientific age, could revive much that was good in the culture of their forefathers. They might translate their intuitive heritage into terms acceptable to modern thinking and thus become guides to a healthier and happier future for all Americans.

ALLEN QUETONE: On the one hand, we have intellectual power which would be understood or practiced by the white man. On the other hand, there is the Indian view of knowledge, or in this sense, the intuitive power of Indian people—their way of living in the natural world, of coping with life. We can break this down into two parts: "Is there still a spiritual or religious feeling among Indian people today, and how does it guide our lives?"

JOSHUA WETSIT: I would say that that old spiritual feeling among our Indians, in the smaller bands like we are of 4000 to 5000 to a reservation, they're losing that pretty fast.

There's one thing we still practice today. After death, regarding the spiritual journey they make, we usually have wakes. Relatives, friends and everyone bring food and they stay up (not every occasion, but most cases). They respect the dead. At the end of four days, after the death of a person, they believe that this person departed from his body and his soul went to the Spirit world. He or she has been over there to see relatives and friends that had gone ahead of him. They had all this that would bring them to the Great Spirit. It's over there and they're settled and meet the people there, and the soul is settled now. They want in behalf of this party to give food—meaning that the dead are having a feast with the relatives and friends. That's the offering they make.

With the peace pipe, when they make that little smudge, purify that and then smoke and offer prayer for the food. The dog is one of the best, most delicious foods they usually use. It's not an everyday food. It's not like white people think, that we just go out and kill any kind of a dog and eat it any time we want. It's just a special meal that's prepared in a certain way. They use that for the purpose of making an offering to the Great Spirit, only on behalf of the deceased person. If there's anything that they want to give, the people that come there, they throw it in, too, and pass it all out and feed everyone. That's one way all come together; that's Indian religion.

We still believe there is a soul after we're dead and our souls are alive in another place.

ALLEN QUETONE: I think Dr. Winkler's question goes deeper into the natural religious mysteries. This power that Indian people knew existed, that they know exists. It is an explanation of the natural power of things and shows the respect and the fear they had of them.

Kiowas had various forms of religious rituals, and it wasn't just one religion. In other words, we all believe this, but in order to express the power, this spiritual power, it was practiced in different ways. We had the Sun Dance in our tribe. We had the Ten Grandmothers. In fact, we still have seven of them remaining and this is still practiced. There is still the respect of these things.

Some individuals had certain powers gained in this spirit quest of the Indian going out to the mountain to receive a message or spiritual power that would build him up to the point of possessing this "thing." How was it used?

ALEX SALUSKIN: The latest Indian dreamers of the Pom Pom were Smaha'la and Koo-ta-ya'hn. One had come back from the dead and the other one had met his spirit because another man had beat him up and had thrown him in the river for dead. He survived that ordeal and came back with a message that by acting like a vicious animal he was acting against himself spiritually. If he thought of killing in order to satisfy his anger against his fellow man, he would lose his life forever—he'd never reach the Great Maker, as they call it in our Indian way over there, because he had committed the unforgivable sin. That was one of his teachings.

The other was that since there were unwritten agreements or contracts, so honesty was taught, and if anyone had a habit of lying, he became an outcast to the tribe. This was to advise the people that this person had become a liar. Then his social standing would drop to the ground and the tribe would not accept any of his promises or other actions.

From this teaching, it was a great honor to have another

23

person point and say, "Well, this young man here, so far he has been upright, has developed a reputation. He is going to be a fine leader." The older people watched him very close because he's been trained under this spiritual guidance, because this one man was responsible for that whole particular band or tribe or many tribes.

One of my first cousins—his name means "Wounded"—was asked by Old Man Saluskin to go hunting. The deer were coming down from the high mountain, snow was driving them out, and they would be down in the lower country, so it'd be easy to get extra meat for the winter. They would get it and prepare it and take it home. That's jerked venison.

So they took some horses and they camped at the place. They said, "Tomorrow this looks like a good place," but it started to show a storm. Rolling clouds came to the mountains. The owl lit on a tree and started to hoot. The old man was busy preparing the meal. He stopped fixing the meal and he told his grandchild, "Well, Grandchild, seems to me that we have to saddle our horses up again. We're going to have to get out of this valley. We just have enough time to get back over the next mountain to get back into the plains, down to the lowland. The deer will be plenty down there when the storm hits here. But it's not going to stop here, it's going to go right on."

My cousin heard that owl hooting, and he noticed his grandpa had stopped to listen. So they saddled their horses as it commenced to get dusk. They rode all night, getting over that hill, and on top of that hill the blizzard was cutting across the mountain. The horses had just enough strength to get over to the east side of the mountain. They got in a good location and stopped there.

Johnny Wildman, this cousin, related that story after Grandpa died. He told me what happened, and he believes from that experience that the old man understood what the owl was saying to him. That's why he hurried back over the mountain to get on the safe side.

Other people, medicine men, could pick up hot rocks. I've seen that—boil two-three gallons of water and stick their hands in the water, put that hot water on their heads and then reach for those hot rocks. Get up and sing their spiritual songs. White man calls it mass hypnotism. But I was there to see it. Many of our people are blessed with a kind of spirit.

I was there to see an old lady take the blood out of a man who was beat up badly. Probably someone threw him down and kicked him and he just looked like he was run through a meat grinder, in bad shape. This little old lady, she stood about ten-fifteen feet away from him and sang her song. She got a bowl of water. She put some of that in her mouth. She stood up and blew it from her mouth, at the same time gesturing towards the body and saying, prayer-like, "Please, through your power take the blood out from that wounded and suffering man." When she blew that mist to the body of that hurt man, the blood came out from his ears, eyes and wherever there was a break of hide. The next day that fellow was walking around. Where did she get that blessing? How did she get it?

That was their secret. The old people never related how they got the power, never said this is the way I acquired it. Just like my grandpa: how did he learn to interpret the owl hoot? So I believe that the blessing comes through from an animal or water or anything that has pity for you; that holds the pity for you because you asked the Holy Spirit, the Great Creator, that I want to be pitied and you get pitied and get blessed.

ALLEN QUETONE: You have had some training by the older Indians, and I think it goes without saying that the rest of these gentlemen have experienced the same type of training when they were growing up. I had some myself, but not to the extent, I'm sure, that most of you have. How have you been able to use or translate this early Indian training? Do you attribute any of your present guidance, your direction of life, to any of this training?

25

ALEX SALUSKIN: I got married about 1923 under Indian ceremony. My wife is strong Indian religion. Our children and grandchildren were taught this Indian philosophy, as you call it, spiritual training. But none of our children went through the process of fasting and fighting the elements when they were children. That's probably where we start to fail in not having this training handed down to our children. Another thing is that the wilderness, the places where I used to go when I was a little boy, every bit of that is occupied now by civilization, even the forest. Whether or not that Spirit which is stronger than I am is still up there and will bless someone else. . .? Anyhow, maybe this is the failure of our race and our generation because we didn't hand this down to our children.

I go to her church and this Pom Pom religion basically says the same thing as what I say. This earth is our mother. When we die, the breast of our mother's body opens so it will receive our bodies back to the earth again. If you have done the right things here, it will go back to the Great Creator from which it had come. You'll return back there where your children are and with those that had been blessed to go back. If you didn't do the right things, you'll only go so far; and if you are already condemned, you'll never go any place. You'll live in misery in the same respect as the crawling insect. When once your body goes into the ground, it shines like a gold piece and the chimes from heaven start ringing, which alerts the Great Spirit that you're coming back. They have seven drums, and they line up with the Indian garment on, and they beat the drums in unison and sing. Each individual has his own songs, which were handed down to him or blessed directly to him who is interpreting the song.

This is the type of religion that I'm associating with now. If I go to a friend over there, I have to go to his church, because I think that if I brought my beliefs in any man's church, I'm only believing that I have one creator, whether it's your church or my church or my friend's church. Because

I'm not going to be influenced, or no one is going to influence my soul, unless I'm the one who's going to. I'm the only one who's responsible for that soul. If I don't do the right thing here, I'm at fault, not him, not the church, not that mountain over there or the sun. This is the way they teach Indian religion. No one is going to influence, no one is going to bring you up to your grave, but yourself.

ALLEN QUETONE: There is one point that ties in with this Indian practice. (I don't like the word "religion" because it has too much a connotation of present-day denominations as we know them in this country.) Thinking of the Indian spiritual world, an experience I had four years ago fits in. I was taking an older Kiowa man to a hearing, and it was quite far away. I had to get up at four o'clock in the morning and meet him at five at his home. He happens to be a priest of these Ten Grandmothers. I got there at five o'clock, and his wife met me at the door. She invited me into their home, and I sat there and visited. She was cooking breakfast, and he was in the other room. Pretty soon I heard him talking. He was talking in Kiowa, but he was talking to somebody, I thought. As he went on a little longer, I began to realize that he was praying. He finished and came back into the room.

The thought I had, and the point I should like to make here on this spiritual concept: I decided the Indian people have a closer personal relationship to this spiritual Indian world. This Indian talked as though someone were in the room, sitting, listening. He was actually praying to the Higher Power.

SYLVESTER MOREY: You yourself felt there was an immediate awareness and connection?

ALLEN QUETONE: Right, and these are the things that need to be strengthened among Indian people, this feeling, this attitude.

I think this is more or less as each of you have experienced, and you've had to make a decision somewhere along the line in the dominant white man's world that you live in as to where or how much of this you are going to forget, how much of this are you not going to practice because of the necessity of life.

We had a discussion last night where I tried to make it clear that when Indians get together like this in their meetings — for instance, a political council of the tribe — the Indian way is a natural process. Every man speaks his piece. Every man says what he wants to. Everybody listens. They deliberate on it. No answer is made at that time. The door, the meeting, is open to anybody: to new ideas, to new people, to the white man if he wants to come in, but it's left to the Indian people sitting and listening to weigh this, evaluate it, to consider what good there is in what has been said. Once the deliberation has been made, then the answer is given. We take part of it, all of it, or none of it.

This was the Indian way of adapting to life in every way, to all the problems that approach Indian people. We still do this. We do it every day in our meetings, in our relationships, in visiting among ourselves.

ALFRED BOWMAN: What has been commented on by Mr. Kindle yesterday: He had stated that the three main ceremonies that became known in the fall of the year, the Fire Dance, the Yeb-be-chai Dance and the Victory Dance (it's what they call the Squaw Dance) — that one use of these dances was upon returning from war. It is going to clear him from all those evils that he had encountered during the war, so that he will again live in peace and harmony with everything that he contacts in nature or with human beings. These rituals and songs don't come about every day or every other week. If they had done something that should not have been done, the spirit of the thing they mistreated would come back and a certain ceremony which would clear them came about.

Just like the two gentlemen said about the puberty ceremony, when a girl comes to womanhood, she had been taught that she would become a mother in time, and she got

28

all the training that she needs to be a successful mother. The gifts that they talked about, both gentlemen, shows that she should also be generous to all those people who are in need, all those that she comes in contact with that need to be helped. That's the origin of that present giving. It's not what is considered in the white man's world as a handout.

On the other hand, youth is taught that he has to go through an endurance test. He has to break the ice to go and bathe himself in that water in the winter time, and then he has to roll in the snow, just like bathing in the water. That is his school: to teach him to endure all the natural elements that he will encounter during his life. Then he is taught that he should never depend on anybody. He is an individualist, and he has to act like that and with respect to everybody and everything he comes in contact with.

GUY QUETONE: The Kiowas believe in possessing the spirit. In order to get the spirit, you have to go to some lonely mountain, take your pipe and no water and no food. You fast there for four days. Pray to nature that he endow you with gifts. If he pities you, you receive the gifts. He also gives you a ritual to go by which you have to obey, and if you disobey the taboos, you're subject to punishment.

I was never a medicine man, but I saw many of them. My grandpa was a medicine man. Many different spirits are gifts, not just one kind. The Kiowa medicine man is not medicine man for all gifts. He doctors certain kinds. My grandfather was a spirit witch doctor. They claim that after a man dies, the spirit continues to live here on earth, roam around. White people say that's your guardian angel. Kiowa say sometimes it goes into the hoot owl, takes possession, and they don't like the hoot owl come around their house. When he comes hooting around my house, I run him away. I don't want his blessing. Whether we believe it or not, you often see some people paralyzed in the face, twisted up. Is it caused by that spirit? So the medicine man has to doctor and fix him up.

Not everybody that goes up there on top of the mountain

four days and nights receives the gift of the spirit. Sometimes you get it and sometimes you don't. You have to put up with the test. It could be a dream and a test, and it could be real.

There's a great big lake, Devil's Lake, that used to be Kiowa territory. Many men went to Devil's Lake to get that gift. Lay down four days and nights. Sometimes that water boils and roars and speaks, and the test comes. If you haven't got the courage to receive the spirit, get scared and run off, you don't get it. You have to hold your ground if you want the spirit.

They tell of one Kiowa-Apache who said, "You people nail me down with stobs on the ground, my feet and my hands, and when the test comes to scare me away, I can't get away and he'll have to give me the gift." The first time the water roared, and he could hear voices in the water. After a while some monster came out, said, "My dear son, you can't get my gift. You have to move, you have to get away. I'll not pity you. I'll not give you a gift." He was nailed down, he couldn't get up. So the water monster went back four nights and tried to move him, and he didn't budge because he had no way, he was tied down.

After the fourth night, before morning light, there came a band of warriors, about fifty, and made a charge on him to take his life. He couldn't escape, so he just left himself to the fate. When they got very near, they disappeared and changed to a flock of geese — flew right over him. They landed in that lake. He thought that he was going to be blessed with the gifts, so he had hopes.

The next night the water began to boil and overflow. Looked like it was going to overflow and drown him. He had no way to get away, he just as well get drowned. Water came and touched his body. He didn't move and the water monster came out and began to speak to him, like we are speaking to each other now. That was nature talking to him.

He said, "You're so determined for the gifts of the spirit, we are going to let you have it. The father wants to speak to you at the bottom of the lake. He asked me to come and get you." So, by magic power the rawhides he was staked with fell off. He followed the water monster and went inside the teepee. There were sitting inside the teepee, all kinds of water varmints, even Mr. Snapping Turtle and all kinds of beavers, otters, alligators, crocodiles and every water monster was in there. They were having a council and the chief said, "Son, I'm going to bless you and give you gifts, so you'll be my medicine man. You'll be endowed with power to cure any kind of disease on earth." So each water monster breathed in his mouth the water gifts, possessed him with that power and gave him his ritual and song. "Take him out," he said. "The geese will take you home."

So they bunched together and he laid across their backs and they flew up, bore him up in the clouds, carried him to the destination of the Indian village. Whooping and yelling, the people were playing Indian ball game. As the geese circled, they was something dark on their backs. The geese circled and landed quite a ways from where the village was on the prairie. When they saw a man walk up, all of them ran to him. Everybody wanted to talk to him, but he said, "No, first you have to make a sweat house. I can't touch any of you and tell you anything until after the sweat house ceremony." So they made a sweat house. For a little while he was inside. Then he was telling the story, how it happened he was possessed with great power and gifts. He could doctor any kind of disease and cure it.

Several years later, the geese were heard coming. "The geese are telling me that my father wants me back into Devil's Lake bottom," he said. "There's a bad disease coming on this earth that I'm not possessed with the power to heal, and that's smallpox. I must go back home. That epidemic of smallpox is coming and I'm not able to doctor that."

Everybody wanted him to stay. They held him. He said, "You sit up with me without sleep, I'll stay; but whenever you get tired and get sleepy, I'm going to leave you." So different ones sat up with him, and after one at a time all went to sleep, he put his tent down and left. The next

31

morning he was gone, but they could see the tracks of the teepee where we went. They followed his pole tracks to where they led into the water. They say that Kiowa made lots of visits over there and lying on their backs they could hear that tomtom beating under the water and the singing of medicine songs. Echoes are there yet today.

That's the way these gifts are. There's a lot of medicine men got gifts different ways. They say you can give this gift to your relatives. If I want my son to inherit my gift, I could give it to him, transfer that power and ritual, and he receives the same gift and he can doctor too. It's been often tried and it's been done.

My grandpa tried to give it to me. He blew me all over. He wore blue beads around his neck all the time, around his ankels and arms. He carried certain kind of medicine feathers and had rituals he used. There was one time, you don't have to believe it, but it's real.

My wife's half-cousin died. They moved everything in the building, took it out. Kiowas believe in destroying everything when one dies. Everything in the house — throw it out, burn it up. We don't want the spirit to come in, so we move new furniture in.

One summer, we were sleeping. The two boys were sleeping in the room where the woman died. It was not too late, maybe about ten or eleven o'clock in the night. Something opened that door — that's what the boys said — and they saw a spirit start to come in. They jumped out of bed and came running in to where I was sleeping.

I took some matches and went into the room. I opened the door, struck some matches to see if I could see anything. When I opened the door, I could feel wind over my face. It passed me. I didn't see anything. I just felt the wind. That night every nerve in my face drawed up; my mouth was way over here, my eyes were down here. I was twisted up. The next morning I started to make a fire to cook. I took a glass of water to drink and I couldn't drink. Old Indians say evil spirit has witched you. You spit and if your spit doesn't go straight, you're already witched. So I tested it. I spit and the spit didn't go that way, it went some other way. I woke my wife. I said, "Look at me." She said, "Nothing wrong with you."

It was Saturday morning. After breakfast I went to Lawton. Walking down the street there was a Comanche boy coming. Before he got to me, he said, "Ha, what's the matter with you? Night man got you. Look at your face." On feeling, I could feel the muscles drawn up. I knew I was twisted, and I went back home. The next morning I had to teach class in Sunday School. That morning about ten o'clock I could speak, but hardly. By eleven o'clock, I told the people, "I have to dismiss you. I can't speak. Something's wrong with me." They said; "We can see your face all right." All went home. I went home.

The next day everybody heard the story and came to visit me. Several men tried to doctor me in Indian. Nobody succeeded. Comanche friends came and wanted to take me to a witch doctor. I said, "No." The third week I was that way, all the folks went to church. I said to my grandson, "We're going to try my grandpa's medicine to see if it works. I am going to try it on myself."

I had all those things that he used in the ritual. I had the beads and crow and prairie hawk feathers and buffalo hide, coal and some other Indian medicine to put in the fire. We put the quilt on the floor, made a fire and went through the ritual, put that medicine in the fire and smoked the feathers. Every time I touched myself, it looked like pins sticking in me. It was the feathers, heated a little, but it was working. After, I told my grandson, "Now I feel better. Look at me."

"Grandpa, it's all right," he says. "You're all right." And that's the way I got my face in the right place again. It all went completely away. After we cleaned up everything, somebody knocked on the door. There was a Kiowa Indian, Frank Saverton. He came in. "I came to see you. I heard you were all twisted up. I don't see any twist about you."

I didn't believe in it, but I tested it and it worked. I don't call myself a medicine man, but maybe grandpa shot it deep enough so it worked.

We Kiowas believe the spirits roam this earth and appear sometimes to relatives. As we know them, good spirits are around you, protecting you, and the bad ones cause you trouble. You white people also say they live on earth and are with you, your guardian angels. We call them ghosts or departed spirits.

Around about 1915, I was very sick and I was in the Indian Hospital at Lawton. All the patients were in a large single room. A Comanche man, Neil, was next to me, near my bed. We often talked about these questions.

One night after all the lights were out — I do not know how long it was, but it must've been sometime after twelve P.M. — I awoke and a few feet from my bed stood a ghost. He commenced to talk to me. First he pointed his finger at me and said, "You. I mean you. You have my pajamas and I come after them. Take them off." I said, "No, the doctor gave them to me. I can't give them to you."

"You will, too. Take them off. They're mine and I'm going to take them." I shook my head, no. "Well, if you're not going to give them up, I will take them off you," — and he started towards my bed.

I said, "No, no."

"All right. I'm taking them off you right now," — and he jumped on me, grabbed my throat. At that point I yelled to the top of my voice. The nurses all heard me and the doctor in charge came running. "What's the matter, Guy?"

I began taking them off. "I want another pair of these pajamas. These belong to that ghost and he wants them. He started to take them off me and choking me. I began to yell for help. Doctor, when you came and put the lights on, he disappeared."

"Oh, Guy, nothing's here. You just had a bad nightmare."

"No. Take those clothes to him, give them to him. I don't want them. Give me another pair," — which they did, and he never bothered me any more.

I have lots of experience stories, not only mine, but other men's, I could tell you. You say these gifts are not real. I say they're real. Kiowas say they're real. The medicine man, you say it's not so, but I know it works.

BEN BLACK ELK: Why we're on earth. It's a Great Spirit created us to be like him. He put us on earth. The white man came, said there's Christianity and we got to live like them. We do it. But in my beliefs, that's to my elders' beliefs, if there's hell, it's on earth. We have happy hunting ground. We die and we go up. There's an Old Lady sits up there. If you're not worthy to go to happy hunting grounds, she pushes you off.

That's why the Indians speak with the spirits. All of us are part of the Great Spirit. When we die we become a part of it. That's the way we believe. So therefore our teepee signifies the universe. That's the symbol of the Sioux.

Nature is something that we believe. We are created by the Great Spirit. He created us and he created the things, even the little ants. All, everything that he created is for my use. We don't order the sun; we don't order the rocks? but there's a Great Spirit. He's so holy we can't face him alone, so we send our voices through the trees, through the things that he created. When I say, "Hau Kola," I send a voice through you to the Great Spirit. That's the idea of this life.

But today it's different. Today we're losing our heritage from the old people that handed down their knowledge. We Indians have religion, brought to the Indians long time. I don't know how far back, but I feel that it was before Christianity. Our people are so old that we know there's a God. We are relatives to the animals and everything in the world, even the little ants. They're our people, too. So we pray to the Great Spirit and when we load that pipe up, it's loaded with everything: the four-leggeds of the universe, the winds of the universe, and the two-leggeds. The Indian humbles himself.

CHAPTER III

EDUCATION AND RELIGION

A number of interesting bits of personal information were disclosed in various unrecorded conversations with the Indians. For instance, Mr. Guy Quetone said he had been at the White House for dinner with three different presidents. He reported in some detail on the menus at these occasions, especially on the small size of White House biscuits. Mr. Quetone as a story teller was one of the greatest. Despite the fact that he had hearing difficulties he took great joy in life and was a very cheerful person to have in a meeting. His son kept him informed on the course of the discussions when he missed points, by writing a vast number of notes for him on a pad that the elder Quetone always had ready at hand.

Mr. Alexander Saluskin has also been a Washington visitor. He was at the inauguration of President Kennedy. Mr. Saluskin is interested in languages, and has been working on his native tongue, the Yakima language, to put it in written form. Although he is over seventy years old, he hoped to spend a year at the University of New Mexico and in that time obtain his A.B. degree. Mr. Saluskin is acquainted with some language professors who have encouraged him to continue his education and to complete his work on the Yakima language.

Mr. David Kindle (Navajo) spoke no English. Mr. Alfred Bowman acted as his very able interpreter. However, Mr. Kindle seemed to understand in a general way what the various speakers were trying to impart. When it came time for Mr. Kindle to speak he told his stories in very liquid and beautiful Navajo phrases. It was a joy to listen to him and his words made a deep impression on the listeners.

Each Indian had something different to say and said it in his own individual way. Also each man had something in his character that was very much alive, and so each one had living information to impart. There was not a moment's lag in any of the conversations.

At the beginning of the previous session, Dr. Winkler felt he had to speak further to the Indians about the problems of youth, as this topic had come up in so many of the more or less private conversations. It may interest white readers to note the concern of the Indians over these problems, as they certainly also concern and puzzle white parents everywhere.

Dr. Winkler's remarks on the causes of the rebellion of youth have been gratefully received by thousands of parents all over the country, just as they were well received by the small group of Indian Elders in Denver. It so happened that he was asked to speak for television on this subject shortly after his return from Denver. Capital Cities Broadcasting Corporation, owner of five television stations, brought eight of its leading correspondents into its Albany, New York, station to interview Dr. Winkler. They discussed the problems of sex, drug addiction, suicidal tendencies, rebellion of youth, marriage, etc., for several days before TV cameras. The resulting series, entitled "A Visit with Franz E. Winkler, M.D.," started with a program called "Sex and the Search for Adventure." The response to it was so positive that the Capital Cities Corporation notified other stations that tapes of the program were available for broadcasting over any station as a public service. Many TV stations have made use of the offer and broadcast the program without commercials. A second program, equally successful, is entitled "What is Happening to the Family".

Dr. Winkler's remarks at the Denver meetings as reported in the last chapter are of course brief and speak specifically to the special problems of Indian youth. What interested the Indians especially and what seemed to arrest the attention of white audiences is the fact that here is someone who really understands the problem of the decline of contemporary culture, the reasons for it and where one has to look for a cure. Knowing the truth about a problem, even though one has not fully achieved the cure himself, brings a sense of relief.

In reviewing the conversations in the last chapter, it is apparent one thing stands out. These Indians have not the slightest doubt of the existence of a supernatural realm. They also feel they know that the individual is personally connected with this spiritual realm, can communicate with it while still on earth, and will become an active part of it after death. Think of the picture created by Mr. Saluskin's statement that after death "once your body goes into the ground, it shines like a gold piece and the chimes of heaven start ringing...."

There is something more than faith in the spiritual world which shines through the statements of these sincere and earnest men. Compare what they said and how they said it with what white people say about life and death and the hereafter. Most whites who have any real interest in the subject frankly admit their doubts; for them there is a vast difference between faith and knowledge. Of course, some are so materialistic as to claim to know that death is the end of everything. But people, even Church people, who have a firm and sure conviction such as these Indian Elders are hard to find.

And yet these Elders who are so sure-footed in their belief, said, one after the other, that their grandparents knew much more about these matters. Their grandparents and great-grandparents knew many secrets that were not passed on or could not be passed on to them.

For this reason, Dr. Winkler urged, as many others have urged, that steps be taken and taken soon to bring more of the traditionally minded Indian teachers into the education of Indian children, before it is too late. Among the others who have urged this is Commissioner Robert L. Bennett.* When the Denver meeting was first suggested, he spoke to Dr. Winkler and Mr. Morey of his interest in finding ways to increase the number of Indian teachers and, in addition, bringing University courses to reservations.

*　　*　　*　　*　　*　　*　　*　　*

Now let us join the next session with the Indian Elders, which dealt still further with the problems of education and

---

*The Hon. Robert L. Bennett (Oneida) served as Commissioner of Indian Affairs from March 1966 to June 30, 1969.

religion.

ALLEN QUETONE: This afternoon's session will be in the same manner. Again this covers our Indian way of life — to use Dr. Winkler's word, the intuitive power that was behind our life, the mystic, the things that guided us and gave us direction and answers to the everyday problems that people had to face to survive.

DR. FRANZ WINKLER: Contrary to generally accepted views, I believe that racial problems rarely arise from differences in outer appearance. The attention paid to skin color or other racial characteristics is, therefore, misdirected, unless one realizes that outer differences are mere indicators of less obvious, but far more important, dissimilarities in thought-life and emotions. An eagle differs from a lion not only in appearance but also in psychological reactions, a fact which makes the king of the air neither better nor worse than the king of the land.

I believe that many of the tragedies of inter-racial strife originate in a mutual ignorance of psychological dissimilarity. Such ignorance prevents people from noticing that promises, commitments, even pacts, may mean entirely different things to the parties involved. For example, certain treaties signed by the white men and considered by the Indians as final were to the former valid only as long as their own political faction remained in power. On the other hand, the red man was often willing to cede land without understanding the white man's concept of ownership, for to his thinking, land could be no man's property.

The psychological gap separating nations and races can be bridged, however, if its existence is realized and respected. For differences in consciousness are necessary for the very survival of the human race. Universal brotherhood, the age-old dream of mankind, can only be achieved when nations and races *maintain* their specific characteristics.

The less its true cause is recognized, however, the more difficult it becomes to overcome the mutual distrust between peoples and races. Paradoxically, it is at times easier for people of different origins to understand one another by gestures and glances than by words. If we are aware of a stream separating us, we may undertake the strenuous labor of wading through the torrent to reach each other. Once, however, we have erected the flimsy bridge of a seemingly common vocabulary, such as the "Pidgin English" of the Far East, we are likely to relax our efforts at real understanding. Yet communication by mere words without further efforts can be misleading, since one and the same word or sentence may convey radically different meanings to the minds of different people.

An ever increasing number of Indians is mastering the English language. But while white and red Americans seem to communicate fluently, they are basically incapable of understanding each other because, unknown to both of them, words, familiar and apparently crystal clear, may actually convey entirely different meanings to the one and to the other.

If these hidden difficulties were fully realized, one of the most formidable barriers between the races would disappear. Yet, unfortunately, differences in consciousness are extremely difficult to understand, since it is a man's nature to assume that any other human being of reason and goodwill ought to think as he does.

In my opinion, the first step toward bridging the consciousness gap between the white and red people would have to be taken by the latter. The reason for this lies in the fact that the Indian has the same intellectual abilities as the white man, while retaining some of the intuitive insight into the essence of things, an insight the white man of today has almost totally lost. This does not mean, of course, that the Indian as an individual is psychologically superior to or morally better than the white man; but he still has at his disposal spiritual resources which the latter can develop only by a painstaking effort to retrain his lost intuition.

When the white man looks at the world, his attention becomes almost fully occupied with the tangible objects in front of him. If he happens to be religious, he may readily admit that somewhere, outside the scope of his consciousness, a spiritual being exists who created these objects. The Indians, on the other hand — at least those who have not yet lost their intuitive heritage — actually sense the *creative* forces still alive behind each created object. Consequently, a certain tree or rock formation may fill an Indian with reverence, regardless of its usefulness or even beauty; for his intuitive perception recognizes in that special object the tangible manifestation of an intangible but still creative force. He therefore considers such objects sacred and will try to preserve them; if need be, he will make his path around them. The white man, meanwhile, can see only a useless rock or shaggy old tree, which he will unhesitatingly remove, if it happens to block the road he wants to build or the lot he wants to clear.

It is easy to see how arguments arising from such differences of awareness can lead to serious resentments on both sides. The white man considers himself at times needlessly opposed in what he regards as progress, and he is therefore inclined to view Indian resistance as vengeful, or at best superstitious. He becomes especially indignant when he had sincerely intended to improve by his standards the living conditions of the very people who opposed him in his action. He is even more baffled by the fact that some Indians may eventually accept the material benefits he offers without ceasing to resent the destruction of natural beauty and tribal tradition that modern "progress" causes.

On the other hand, what is hard for the proponents of a welfare state to understand is the following: Almost every human being can eventually be persuaded to accept material benefits at the expense of spiritual values, yet deep down in his heart he will never forgive his "benefactor" for creating conditions that make him lose his self-respect. (This is the

41

true reason, by the way, why so many white children turn against their wealthy parents. While taking material gifts for granted, they come to hate themselves and their parents for depriving them of inner strength. It is, therefore, not surprising that suicidal tendencies, hippiedom and the misuse of mind-changing drugs are most prominent among children of wealthy and materialistic parents.)

Some elders among the Indians are still aware of the fact that happiness, inspiration and purpose in life depend on an inner awakening. This awakening was sought and often found by the Indian on his "spirit quest." However, this quest required not only preparation on the part of the youth himself but also a proper natural environment.

Those among us who minimize the importance of external conditions of inner transformation need only remember how much we all depend on the right environment for spiritual experience. People with a true understanding of nature will often find a certain interplay of the elements essential for attaining religious communion. The sacred groves of the Greeks and Romans were no less calculated to unlock the gateways of the human heart than were the sacred places where Indian youths discovered their true selves and their mission in life. Desecration of such sacred places, although often unintentional, has inflicted deeper wounds on the Indians than some of the worst political injustices. For the disappearance of such sanctuaries has left a vacuum which nothing the white man has to offer will fill.

Economic opportunities, modern education, health care, are certainly important, but they alone can give neither spiritual meaning nor happiness to youth. Yet seriously as the white man may have sinned against his red brother, against nature, and even against himself, many of his failings must be excused because of his lack of intuitive wisdom. For conditions beyond his control have caused him to trade the deeper wisdom of the heart for the superficial cleverness of the brain. This is why we are appealing to you for help. It is a help that you can give only when you learn to translate your wisdom, which may be sleeping but is still alive, into words the modern intellectual can comprehend. Unless you do so, the illness of this great country will worsen, not only for the white man, but also for your own children.

Education should not come only from professors. What your uncles or older cousins have once taught your fathers, can still be revived for the sake of future generations. But there is no time to lose, for most of those who still have knowledge of the old ways are well advanced in years. Should the last ones die without translating their ancient wisdom into concepts of today, all that was good and wise in Indian culture may die with them.

ALEN QUETONE: This is the second part of today's subject and the question is, "How is it possible to teach today's children the old Indian way, or the intuitive way? In other words, how to modernize or modify this old way or translate it into language that young people can understand today and use in solving their problems, man's problems?"

SYLVESTER MOREY: Mr. Saluskin, you were telling this noon how your uncle taught you when you were young, and of your close connection with nature and what it developed within you.

ALEX SALUSKIN: In our tribal custom, which was handed down to my grandfather, Chief Saluskin Wee-al-wick, each of his children were assigned to a tutor, like he had been by his grandparents, so that each child, each of his descendants, should be trained by an expert. These experts were proficient in hunting and everything for survival, as well as teaching the blessing of the Great Creator. I was assigned to my uncle and his name was Twi-nant in Indian name, in English they call him Billy Saluskin. So he and his wife had undertaken to bring me under their wing for a season. (This was after I had one year of schooling.)

My grandfather came and asked my father if I would make a trip with them to the mountains where they hunt for deer, as well as mountain sheep, and gather huckleberries. They caught salmon from the spawning beds there and dried them for their provisions while they were staying in the mountains. Naturally, they depended for their livelihood on what they could catch and kill, as well as catch small fish from the streams.

When we began, first I was to learn how to control my horse, which was given to me with a complete outfit, as well as a gun. Then we came to the first camp. Early in the morning my uncle started to assume his responsibilities, got me out of bed, and he says, "Nephew, let's hurry down to the creek. It's my duty now to train you, to equip you with the wisdom and knowledge that I had acquired. First of all, we're going to go down to this swift stream and we're going to plunge in that stream and we will disturb the old lady." (We referred to the stream as an old lady.) "We'll disturb her and the old lady will rub' you down and soothe up your sore muscles and give you an endurance for the rest of the day." I knew I had to do the things that I was told. We went down and we stripped off and jumped into this swift water, very cold. We stayed in the water until my body was numb. We came up and pranced around, jumped up and down to get our circulation going. We put on our clothes and by the time we got back to the camp, the breakfast was ready.

Again we were taught how to care for the horses and how to handle them. As we traveled, the same processes were conducted until we reached our destination.

As soon as we reached our destination, I was told that the sweat house and the hot rocks which were prepared for the sweat house were blessings taught and handed down from the Great Spirit. This hot water caused by cold water on the hot rocks would cleanse you and purify your scent, so the wild animals wouldn't detect you. You would have the scent the same as the fir bough and reeds that grow in the mountains. So naturally I had to believe that this was the case. I followed through this system and we had to do this every morning about three o'clock while we were in the mountains.

At the end of our trip, I was wiry; I could walk probably for days and weeks if I had to. I had gone through my course of training for survival. I learned every herb, root, berries and how to take care of them. This kind uncle of mine and his wife took time to explain these things step by step. They didn't leave one thing untold and it was shown physically to me, then asked me if I could do it.

After we reached the mountain, my uncle killed a bear. The old man, my grandfather, had told the other man, "You boys better go back down there and take care of him (the bear). We'll just have to let somebody stay down there and watch it all night." You know who got the assignment! I got the assignment to watch that bear all night.

Like I said yesterday, the marriage is through Indian custom. They never abandon their family under that religious marriage. But these young people now, like the gentleman says here, since World War II they don't want that any more. Yet we have, I would say, about ten percent, maybe fifteen percent, of our Indians still on the Yakima Reservation, still onto their Indian religion and teaching.

ALLEN QUETONE: How do they get this to their young people, to this ten percent?

ALEX SALUSKIN: Through their families. Each of these old people had a family: daughter or son, they still hang onto their beliefs. These little fellows are taught under that religion by their participating, right from the little fellow on up.

ALLEN QUETONE: Supposing you were chosen as a teacher to translate some of these things you have said, to conceptualize this so you could make the young people understand what you are saying or what you would like for them to know, would you have to form a system, or would you follow the old pattern that you experienced?

ALEX SALUSKIN: I believe you would have to set up a system. May I add just one more point there which I went

45

through when my parents were living.

When we were children, one time about five or six of us took our horse swimming. We used him as a sort of ferry boat. A few of us would get on him and let him take us across the water, and finally we got that horse so tired swimming, he almost drowned. We thought we had done something bad, so we turned him loose, but the horse got sick. He didn't pull out of it for a couple of weeks and we couldn't use him any more. The grandfolks wondered what was wrong with the horse but nobody would say anything. We weren't volunteering any information, but it was the responsibility of the young boys and girls in those days, if they were asked, they would have to tell the truth. One girl was asked, "What were you doing with the horse down there?"

"We were using him to swim across the river and when we all got across, we'd come back again. We got him tired and almost lost him in the river." The mother of that girl went to report. Nothing was said then, but we were festering our little mischiefs. One group did something else and another group did something, and things were piled up.

After construction of the long houses of a new village, there was a ceremony to whip these little fellows that had been mischievous for a certain period of time. Each family came and had a report. How many children were involved in this mischief? And we have to say we were. How about this other mischief that was committed? A lot of them were in that too. No one denied it, because they were asked. They were taught honesty. The result was that a hired whipper delivered the punishment. He lined you up, tied the willow rods together, about seven. He let you kneel down in front of all the families, relatives and old folks. That fellow brings his whip up and right across your back just as hard as he could. By about the third blow, you don't feel anything. That was what they give you — three. Some of those smart ones think, "If I turnover and start to whimper, they'll take pity on me and won't whip me." That was worse on them, as that whip man was going to let that punishment come down. All received the same, even the one that was good enough to report us.

The philosphy of that was that if you're playing and someone commences to suggest some mischief, you know somebody is bound to have to tell, somebody of our group is bound to tell, and we'll get a licking. Let's not do it.

JOSHUA WETSIT: We cannot teach our children. They have white teachers, and the children get so that they don't care to learn anything from home. Although I know most of our Indian people among the Assiniboine and Sioux, where I am there, insist on pushing and urging their children to go and try and compete with the whites. Even though they don't have much schooling themselves, they tried hard so that those children could make their grades every year.

When we're speaking about getting back to our days of Indian life, it's pretty hard to make them understand. We have to put it in their language, that would be understandable by common people. In order to get them to practice that, we have to teach them so it could be something that would be interesting. Lot of times they don't understand it, and they lose interest. It's something you've got to offer, the goal that we're working for.

I picked up a paper not long ago and read an article regarding education: a professor teaching among white people in public schools, teaching religion to American people. I suppose we all know about how they've been struggling about the religion in the public schools. In our constitution it is open for freedom of religion, but we don't permit them to use even one short prayer before they start the day of schooling. On the other hand, when any public officer takes the oath of office, they raise their right hand to the Great Spirit or the God. Congress, they have prayers. They have certain one come in to say prayers.

But our Indian religion is all one religion, the Great Spirit. We're thankful that we're on this Mother Earth. That's the first thing when we wake up in the morning, is to be thankful to the Great Spirit for the Mother Earth: how we live, what it produces, what keeps everything alive.

I know my old father — died about twenty years ago, almost a hundred years old — he never neglected his thanks early in the morning when he'd be out and the sun came up, shining — that's the eye of the Great Spirit. No matter what he's doing, certain times, he looked up, just before it got into the middle of here in the sky — that's the throne of the Great Spirit. When the sun got about there, noon, he stopped, just for a few seconds, gave thanks to the Great Spirit and asked to be blessed. Then again when the sun was going down, he watched that until it got out of sight. Those are the things I always think is wonderful when we're talking about our Indian life.

My father was a medicine man. He did lot of doctoring and he cured lot of sickness. I don't know how he did it. I asked him to show me how to do it. You got to make an offering. You got to make a suffering to show your faith that you're sincere. You got to know what the power is you're going to use, what kind of bird or animal. Even from flowers or something that's pretty, you can never tell what you can use.

Every man is born under a certain thing. He may not know how to do many things, but there's something a man is going to be expert at. If he practices it, he can use it. He has a power to use it.

So to speak, this is quite a subject we're on and I hope something can be worked out to interpret that, so we could use it for the good of our country. The way the young people are going, it's not so good. That's what we have to protect. The jet age makes a lot of things different now from what it used to be. Time for a change. Like that travel I was telling you about — I saw them travel and then today in the jet age, that's entirely different. It is the same in the way of life, too. We have to make these new ways, new methods, all that is coming about. Somebody said, "We get education, things are going to get so that it won't be much problem." But it's different, and the more education we have, our problems are getting worse and bigger all the time.

ALLEN QUETONE: You have commented well on some of the problems that would be faced by Indian people who forget or do not use this intuitive power, intuitive or Indian way. As Dr. Winkler explained earlier, the intuitive way is from the inside, which explains the natural knowledge that Indian people have. There was no formal schooling; instead, a personal training had to relate you to the world about you. I think this is part of the quest that we have here.

Today Indian people who are still holding on to the remnants of their Indian way, at least try to find a manner of expressing this Indian way of life in today's world. They have done it in their own native way.

This is a method or idea that has to be worked out if a new way is found to strengthen and perpetuate our Indian life. It's difficult for young people. For instance, Kiowa people — and I'm sure all Indian people — teach their young people to be patient, especially among their elders. It's a quality that has high importance in Indian life. You're taught this from the very beginning. But then today, the young Indian has to go out into the world and compete. The outside world is a competitive, aggressive world which will leave behind the man that has patience, that stands back and lets the next man have the way. So in the modern world there has to be a balancing, a reconciling of ways.

These are the things that need to be deliberated on by Indian people. Some of these are realities that have caused our Indian way of life to suffer, because it's hard, especially for the younger Indians, to practice some of these things in a different setting.

BEN BLACK ELK: That's the point we have to teach our children. They have to be proud they're Indians. We raise our children that way; but these kids raise their kids, it is modern. In the modern time, it's different. We have to go accordingly, and we have to teach our children to be proud because they're Indians.

We were created by a Great Spirit. We have a primitive way of living and we survive. We didn't know what the dollar was, whiskey was, and coffee was. That's the point we have to go back to for our answer. We have a culture of our own so great, it's greater than any culture in the world. This honesty, that's the way we have to teach our children to go forth.

ALEX SALUSKIN: As one of the Indians who had direct communications with the past, especially from the old people, I'm hopeful my contribution could be of some help in bringing the light to the Christian world. We have heard a great deal about how, when the Europeans came to this continent, they claimed that we were totally savage. We didn't know right from wrong. To my own belief, from what I could learn and from what I have learned from my old people, the Indians were worshipping all the time. There was direct contact with the spirits from the heaven, and they knew what was right and what was wrong.

DR. FRANZ WINKLER: It seemed hardly necessary to bring up in a formal manner the topic of religion, since in almost all that you have said a religious mood prevails. This fact has made a deep impression on Mr. Morey and me. Among white people, a religious atmosphere is usually totally absent unless the topic under discussion is religion itself, because religious and secular matters are kept strictly separated. Yet for anyone who believes in the Great Spirit, no problem of any significance, even in the fields of science or psychology, or in social and racial questions, can be solved without some relation to the primary cause of all things. Naturally I am in favor not of constant Bible quoting, or any sentimental piety, but of a mood of awe, together with the knowledge that no problem can be truly solved by considering only its surface appearance.

I am, of course, not under the illusion that all Indians think and feel as you do, but I am nevertheless deeply impressed by the fact that people from such widely scattered tribes, in several instances unknown to one another, could from the very first day be united by a mood that I can only call religious in the true sense of the word.

For the sake of the many people who will be interested in your religious views, I should like to translate into conceptual terms what I believe is your mutual view. Even when saving time is of the essence, philosophical concepts must be at least sketchily traced back to two principles, the historical and the psychological. At the time when the great creeds were born, man's relationship to his Creator was based on intimate, intuitive experience. Buddha, Moses, Jesus, Mohammed and their disciples unmistakably spoke from immediate experience, not from theological tenets; and so it was with the founders of the Indian creeds. That creeds differ is inevitable, since the people to whom they spoke were not only imperfect but also so constituted that they had to visualize God from different angles. Nor is there a real contradiction even between monotheistic and polytheistic religion, since all creeds conceive of the *one* Creator and His countless servants. Whether you call those servants gods, angels, devas or hierarchies makes little difference. Yet in order to perceive the creative principle behind the created universe, one must possess an ability which the Romans called *intuitio* which means the ability to look into the intangible source behind the tangible surface. Sense perception, on the other hand, makes us aware of the outward but passing world.

There are cultures that are predominantly intuitive. While people belonging to such cultures are aware of the Great Spirit, they often pay too little attention to the material world and therefore run the risk of falling victims to more earthly civilizations. The latter display a greater ability to deal with the practical problems of life but, in turn, they are in danger of losing sight of spiritual values. Either is incomplete and cannot survive for long unless it creates the right balance by joining forces with its counterpart. Destiny usually brings about the chance for such an alliance, but it leaves it to the free will of man to accept or reject the opportunity.

The American Indians are a predominantly intuitive people and therefore capable of sensing the spiritual core of man and of nature. On the other hand, the Europeans who conquered this country were highly sense-oriented. True, they brought along their creeds and adhered to them, often in almost fanatical loyalty, without realizing that fanaticism and religious intolerance are already indications of intuitive blindness.

The Indians who enjoyed a much more intimate relationship with the Great Spirit were intrigued by the newcomers' forceful assertions that they had specific and detailed knowledge of God's nature and will. They were not aware that this "knowledge" no longer stemmed from immediate experience but was based on various interpretations of an insight already lost.

The Judeo-Christian message brought to this shore by the white man appealed strongly to the religious interest of the Indians. All the greater was the disappointment when the red man, seeking universal brotherhood in a religion of peace, discovered that the various Christian factions mistrusted and often fought one another. I believe that this disappointment had contributed greatly to the mistrust the red man feels toward the white. If, however, the Indian understood fully the difference in consciousness mentioned before, he would see that the white man's divisiveness and strife in religious matters does not so much stem from insecurity or ill will as from tragic loss of the intuitive preception that unifies. Here, a unique opportunity may exist for you, or at least the wisest among you, to revive religious *awareness* in the great but no longer vividly experienced creeds of the white man. Such a deed would make the Indian the true victor in the centuries-old contest between the red and white man. It would be a victory in the truest sense of Christianity.

Some of the Indian Elders who attended the conference. Left to right: Allen Quetone, Kiowa, Chairman; Sidney Carney, Seneca; Alexander Saluskin, Yakima; Alfred Bowman, Navajo; David Kindle, Navajo; Guy Quetone, Kiowa; Ben Black Elk, Oglala Sioux.

Dr. Franz E. Winkler, President of the Myrin Institute of Adult Education, is a prominent New York physician and psychologist who, along with his medical practice, has long been concerned with education at all levels. Dr. Winkler became interested in American Indians through a story by Karl May, whose fictional stories have left a lasting impression on countless Europeans. In the later years of his life, Dr. Winkler rediscovered the image, which as a boy he had formed of the red man, in the still living ideals of the Indians he met through professional and social contacts. Dr. Winkler is the author of a remarkable book, *Man: the Bridge Between Two Worlds.*

Mr. Sylvester M. Morey, Chairman of the Myrin Institute for Adult Education, was instrumental in bringing about the conference with the Indian elders. Mr. Morey recently retired as Board Chairman of Geyer, Morey, Ballard Advertising Agency. For ten years he served on the Board of the Rudolf Steiner School, New York City, and was a director of the Waldorf Educational Foundation that is closely connected with the Waldorf School of Adelphi University. Mr. Morey, a Dartmouth alumnus, has long been interested in American Indians. His lecture, "American Indians and our Way of Life," was published in the Proceedings of the Myrin Institute.

Rev. Guy Quetone, a Kiowa Indian from Oklahoma (left), is a Methodist minister who has preached in more than a dozen missions and churches in Oklahoma. He has held various offices in connection with Indian affairs and has served as an interpreter in Washington. Rev. Quetone's stories were among the best. To his right is Ben Black Elk, an Oglala Sioux.

David Kindle, a Navajo, came to the conference from Shiprock, N.M. Deeply religious and a student of human nature, his vivid stories were always much to the point.

Alexander Saluskin from Toppenish, Washington, is much interested in languages and has been working to put his native tongue, the Yakima language, in written form. Although over seventy, he plans to attend the University of New Mexico and obtain his A.B. in language.

CHAPTER IV

ORIGIN OF INDIAN PEOPLES

By now the reader may have noticed that the discussions became freer on succeeding days, and that the men spoke more easily and openly than before. This was especially true of the meeting reported in the last chapter.

To one who was there it was as though he had watched a flower slowly open. The long conversations between the individuals, either in a group or privately, over a period of several days had caused a warmth of feeling to develop. Gradually, everyone began to grasp the true purpose of the meeting. As a result, each participant realized he could open his mind freely to the others in trustfulness and with full enthusiasm.

It was this kind of atmosphere that permitted Dr. Winkler to speak to the Indians so frankly about the gap in understanding that has always separated the white man from the red. His explanation of why such a gap always exists between nations and races was followed closely by all present. And his unexpected statement that it is the red man who will have to take the first step in bridging the gap of consciousness between white and red was accepted without any sign of disagreement. This was one of several concrete suggestions made in Denver as to how the red man can help the white man in today's world.

Mr. Saluskin's description of his youth and early training was given with equal candor, as was Mr. Wetsit's report about his father and his description of his father's deeply spiritual nature.

If one projects oneself into the pictures Mr. Saluskin painted of his early training in practical and moral affairs, one can begin to understand what it means to be an Indian—that is, an Indian trained under the old moral code. It is good to have such records.

Mr. Wetsit's pictures of his father and his father's daily

routine of worship were closely connected with another one of Dr. Winkler's suggestions as to how the red man can help the white man. This suggestion also was quite unexpected. At first glance, it may seem strange that he should have told the Indians that they, and other Indians like them, are the very people who could help revive *religious awareness* in this country. But Mr. Wetsit had just described religious awareness in the Indian's sense of this term; and everything that happened in Denver during the Indian Elders' conference was surrounded by an immediate and personal awareness of a divine world. All meals started with the saying of grace—each Indian taking his turn. Most conversations sooner or later turned to some topic that disclosed reverence for higher powers. Those who know Indians true to their native culture will understand why Dr. Winkler made this suggestion. With these Indians reverence is a part of their whole being, not just a part of their thought life, to be turned on some days and off others. And now we return to Mr. Quetone for the next discussion.

ALLEN QUETONE: This morning's session will be on the origin of Indian people. Beginning will be the representatives of the Navajo Tribe, Mr. Kindle with Mr. Bowman as interpreter.

DAVID KINDLE: The legend runs this way. The Indian people had come from the bottom world. The reason for their emergence to this present sphere was that there was a flood in that area and to get away from the depth of the water they first tried the pine tree. It started to grow, but it didn't grow high enough to get them to safety. So the next thing was a cane, the big jointed kind. That was tried with a prayer plume tied to it. It started to grow and it grew to this present sphere of habitation.

This is, figuratively speaking, the story of the emergence of those beings at that time, the animal kingdom, animal people, coming up to the surface. It is known to the Navajo people as the First Man, the First Woman and also the Great Spirit, the

Communication Talking Spirit. He is the Great Spirit that made this plan to have these animal people emerge onto this present world.

When the people reached to the safety place, up to the ceiling of the sky, the Coyote Spirit first went out to explore and he dug into the surface and could not make it. He came back and reported that he had failed to dig into view of what kind of world we're coming to.

So the next spirit is the Spirit of Badger. He started to dig and could not make it. Then came the third one, the Locust. When the Locust came out, he viewed the land and there was water all over. He sees the only little place where they could sit themselves was on this mountain, La Plata Peak.

There were monster birds who were governing the four corners of this new world. They are known as the White Lake Bird Monsters, and they saw that someone was there in their domain. The one that sits in the East came by to investigate what had happened. He saw someone there and he splashed water into its face, but this Locust never winked. That was the determining thing that this monster bird was trying to do, to have him wink and scare him away, but the Locust didn't wink. The one from the West did the same thing. The one from the South did the same thing. The one from the North did the same thing. The Locust didn't wink, and that is the first phase of this winning of the new land. The Navajo people know to this day that the Locust Spirit does not wink, as we do with our eyes.

This is giving the high points of that emergence story that the Navajo people have in their legend.

This monster bird that was governing the East portion of this new land came a second time and brought two arrows. One was feathered with the black feather of an eagle and one with the light-colored feather of an eagle. Two arrows were left there, and they were to contest to know who would be entitled to this new land. This monster bird shoved the black feather arrow up from his bottom-side and out of his mouth

55

without hurting himself. The light-feathered arrow he put in his mouth and pulled it out from the bottom-side of himself and threw it in front of him, challenging this new person that had come in sight, this Locust. "If you can do what I did, if you win that, the land is your area; you won it from me."

The tug of war began there. "You did that where there is already a natural opening on both sides of your body. You should be the one that should do what I'll do." Then the Locust raised up his heart and put that black-feathered arrow in from his right side and the light-colored feather arrow in on the left side, and he kind of wiggled and pushed them in there and drew each through. "Now, If you do this, the land will be yours, but if you don't, then it's mine." He threw the arrows in from of him. The bird spirit that challenged this Locust Spirit knew that he lost again. He never said another word. He just went away.

Then the body of water that was on this new world, the dam broke to the East, to the West, to the South, to the North. It all ran off the surface of the earth and it became the ocean that skirts the continent now.

When the land was won and the water was taken out four ways, then the land started to appear. The sacred mountains were the first places visible on this new continent. It's put on the east side there to govern the Navajo people. This is the foundation on the east side and Mount Taylor is on the south side; this is San Francisco Peak on the west side and La Plata Mountain on the north side. (Mr. Kindle passed around large photographs which showed these mountains.) It is symbolic. Those are the braces of the Navajo Nation and within their bounds our Navajo Nation has its home. When the land was won and came into our possession, that's the way we were placed with the Great Spirit.

We have a high respect for the female. Our first language after these holy mountains were placed, called this, the land that we were to live on, Mother Earth. We didn't call it a man. And water which is so essential to life we call it Mother

Water, and Mother Salt, Mother Mountain.

I have placed before you the fundamentals of the Navajo people and I'm coming now to the origin of how they came about. It took place on one of those barren mountains; as the legend goes, this is the cradle of the Navajo Nation. They had seen some unusual things on one of these peaks. This is the "Gum in Door Knob." It's a little peak there south of where is now the Navajo Dam. It's way out on top of surrounding country. They saw the clouds were always on it, kept on like that for four days. Then the Spirits were worried about what had happened. Nothing like that had they seen prior to this time. There must have been a communication there.

They investigated and they found a baby girl on this certain peak. The First Man and the First Woman that came with the animal kingdom from the bottom or the emergence place, they're the ones that found the baby.

The baby grew from day to day — as we would say "years" now. Every day was something like a year. When the baby was found, they came to this mesa, and I have been up there to see and it still can be distinguished. There was a place of a home there at some unrecorded date. We were told that that's the place where the baby was brought to be raised.

The child grew up rapidly by days. When she became a young woman, she did the necessary work in the home. They had to bring in the wood on their backs and she was out one day to get a bundle of wood. She picked up the wood and put it in a bundle. She couldn't lift it. What at other times was easy for her to throw on her back and carry home, this time was heavy for some reason. Four different times she tried to lift it, and those four different times she took off some wood. "Maybe I overload myself with my load." Even as she lightened the load, it was too heavy. Seems like somebody was holding it down. The fourth time when she looked around, she saw a person standing there—a young man. She found out it was the fungi in the form of a man.

Upon looking on that young man, she fell in love with

57

him, and they were married. She bore two boys to him that are the sons of the Sun God. Today it's known among the Navajo people that one is the monster or enemy killer. He's the first boy. The second one, we call him the God of Water. It looks like they emerge from two different sources, but that's not so. They are the boys of the Sun God and of that Changing Woman, the mother. Why! She can be a middle-aged woman or a young lady—she has that power to be any of those stages.

I'm just bringing out the highlights. There are lots of details in connection with every part of the legend, but I'm getting to the origin of the present Indian people.

After things were settled down, the First Man and the First Woman and that Talking Spirit, the Talking Communication Spirit, and this Changing Woman were discussing how to people the new world and what to do about this vast land that had become theirs.

When they were discussing where to get the people for this land, they got into a quarrel. They had one white ear of corn, and one yellow ear of corn with twelve rows of kernels on each ear. The white corn would be the man and the yellow corn would be the woman. Of course this was done in a mystic way: Things were spread out and covered, and prayers were made, and of these twelve rows of kernels on the white corn, it became six men, and of the twelve rows on the yellow corn, it became six women. There were twelve persons, six pairs.

It has been told that one can see the place where this has taken place. They say that the fort type of hogan still can be seen some place there. It's been brought out from generation to generation that it still is visible, but he (Kindle) personally has not explored that.

When these six pairs of people were made to live on this new world, they moved around at will. They were still together and they would go from one place to the other, until they drifted down and across the Rio Grande to the

58

east, following the mountain range. Seasonal drifting is the kind of determining factor for these people—to move about—and they came to the end of the mountain range on the east. Lot of those couples, they wanted to stop and talk things over, but one of them left the party there. They just kept on going—one man and one woman going east all the time. They went out of sight to that vast plains area. They became the Plains Indians. Just by a kind of democratic process, they chose their own way and they lived the way they wanted.

One pair, a man and a woman, left the crowd. I believe that it actually happened because those people there and we have almost the same profile. Our language in places almost comes together to where we would understand it. Especially the rhythmic part of it, it runs along the same plane.

From the twelve, two of them went away, which leaves ten people who were still together. Of course this took years and years. They turned about and came down again to the Sandia Mountains. Two others stayed in the mountains there, and that is the origin of these other Apache people there. They liked that mountain country, so they stayed there. They were not forced to go along with the others.

They were minus two more people, which leaves them eight. These eight were still together. When they were moving west again, they crossed the Rio Grande River and two of those people, a man and a woman, tarried there. These are the ancestors of the Pueblo people. This leaves three couples.

When they were coming back to their old habitat where Navajo Dam is now, getting close by, two of them didn't like to come home with them, so they left to the south, a man and a woman. We understand they were the San Carlos Indians and the White Apache Indians; they're the parents of those groups of Indians there.

Starting with twelve people, just four people came back to the original Navajo country. When four people came there, two went on ahead, didn't stop there. They moved to the north part of the country, which is the Jicarilla Apache area adjoining us now at the present time. Their reservation is not too far from the Navajo Reservation.

That lets just those two people, the Navajo people, come to where they are residing now—that's Navajo Nation country there, under those four sacred mountains. (Mr. Kindle's photographs, which were spread on the table, showed these mountains.)

According to the Indian people, we originated in this country which is now known as the United States. This is speaking for all the Indian people. We didn't come from any place, and the Indian people were originally here and they're still living here. These fair-skinned cousins of ours migrated from across the ocean some place. They have come from other countries, to move in here to live in our country.

I think we owe a credit to this white race because they came from across the sea and moved into this new world. They have come with the skill, ingenuity and scientific development. What has been placed here by the Great Spirit for the Indian people—for instance, take the trees—these white people come in and they made a lot of useful things out of them. They have built sawmills, boards to build houses and homes, bridges and conveyances of every kind. I think we owe a great gratitude to this white race from the standpoint of the Indian philosophy.

Even with this ingenuity and his inventiveness of everything of every shape and form, the white man is lacking one thing. He has lost track of his Creator. He has forgotten his Maker. I think that the Indian people have not lost that respect for their Creator, the Great Spirit, and what has been placed to govern our lives in this new world. The Great Spirit has left certain fundamental laws for us that we have to go by and live accordingly.

That scientific development that the white man has developed for himself at first was for the benefit of the mankind, but now he is to the point where he has developed an awful weapon, atomic bomb. That is the danger that is confronting us at the present day: the knowledge of inventiveness up to the point where he's going to develop an awful weapon that would kill all the life on earth. What will become of this country that we love, the country that was placed here for us to live in, enjoy, where we can follow the dictates of the Great Spirit? Are we going to lose it?

The white race has forgotten its Creator which the Indian people still retain. Our Great Spirit, the Talking Communication God, he's not only the God of the Navajo people but is the God of every living human being on this earth. Symbolically speaking, the sky is like the roof of a home, and the earth is like the interior of a home, which, if you stretch your imagination, is universal. We're lacking communication between races, which our Great Spirit meant for us: to come back and communicate between races.

Our next thing is to give every living person a home and a place to live. I think that is meant for all mankind. We're not doing that. We're holding some things that other races of people could enjoy. They're not getting their full share of it, of what our Great Spirit intended for us to share between ourselves.

We have said something about the white corn, the yellow corn, blue corn, mixed corn of all colors. They all have pollen, and our offering to the Great Spirit is this corn pollen. Every vegetation has this pollen. Pollen is the symbolic offering; it scatters itself far and wide, universally. I think it is meant by our Great Spirit for us to use the pollen as symbolic offering, particularly for the Navajo. Other nationalities don't respect that, but we Navajo people still respect that—our offering to the Great Spirit.

That's the offering the pollen, that we use for prayers that happiness and beauty and blessing may abound to ourselves, our family, our people, and people all over to the ends of the earth. It's not just here, it's a universal offering. If we offer blessing from the Great Spirit, it does not concern only us

61

here that are present; it will go beyond to the ends of the earth. Wherever they will contact from here on, they will get the same share, is the way their prayers run.

Because people in general disregard their Maker—the Great Spirit that governs this world—that's why this war is on, that's why even some of our people, our grandchildren, are over there on the battlefields in foreign countries. If they could only recognize that there is a Higher Being, a Greater Great Spirit, I think those things could have been avoided and not talked about. As I stated before, because the inventor, the man that uses his scientific knowledge, has developed things up to the point that they'll just blow off the face of this earth—because he doesn't recognize that there is a Creator and a Higher Being that governs this world and the lives of each of us.

(Here Mr. Kindle stood up, drew from his pocket a small packet of corn pollen. As he talked, he held up the pollen.)

This is symbolic thinking. Just imagine this corn pollen: We use this as offering. Maybe the Great Spirit doesn't need it, but for us it's just the thing. We know we should try to offer what little we have, the pollen which is needed for all vegetation. One plant communicates with another by pollination. Even the worms, even those little ants down there, know this. Pollination is the sign of the growing of the harvest crop or anything that needs pollination; then the fruit comes following that.

(At this point Mr. Kindle blew the corn pollen from the palm of his hand to show how the Navajo does it—how the pollen is carried by the air and connects one part of the land with another and is a symbol of how love can connect one man with another. As he finished, he dipped the fingers of his right hand into the corn pollen and rubbed it on the front of Dr. Winkler's jacket, and then he rubbed pollen on his own chest. It was a graphic demonstration expressing the fact that men are brothers and that pollen not only connects plant with plant but also represents human love.)

GUY QUETONE: Is there still an Indian intuition, religion, religious or spiritual feeling, among Indians in today's world? To get to the bottom of that, we must find whom we're talking about, the Indians. Where did this Indian come from? The spirit he possesses, where did he get this spirit? What is his belief and reason for his existence on earth? We don't know way back 4000 years ago, but the white people have the history. They call it in the Bible a creation. The Indians don't understand that "in the beginning." They have ideas and creation stories of their own. Whether it's so or not, it was not written in history.

Our people, the Kiowas, go back many years and had intelligence enough to have an Indian calendar, Kiowa calendar. In the 1900's the last custodian of that calendar passed away. For years and years back, it had been carried on and handed down to Indians. Relatives inherited that calendar and continued to make a record.

The Kiowas have two creation stories. I will relate one of them.

There were inhabitants on this earth at the beginning of this Kiowa story, as told to the descendants of the Kiowas. The Creator asked all races to be at the great fountain where the water was clear as glass and very deep. The proper offer was made to all by the Creator: that the one that made a dive into the water would live there always. Under the surface of the water were all kinds of sharp instruments reaching almost to the top of the water, including spears, swords, daggers and other sharp materials. All the races accepted the offer, but just before the dive they all changed their minds, as it was deadly to make the dive. At last a Kiowa made the plunge. The waters parted and the sharp spears all changed to bullrushes, water lilies and cat-tails. The sacred waters parted to form an island (which is America) with oceans all around it. "Indian, this is your country. You can live here always in peace. The others will live elsewhere." This was his reward.

Somewhere in this island there was an Indian village, and

the chief's daughter was a princess who was very much loved. She was never allowed to touch the ground, was always carried or walked on carpets. The girls were playing near the creek as usual, where there were many pine trees, and one suggested, "Let's get the princess to play with us." They went to get permission for her to play with them. The folks said she could not touch the ground. "We will see to that. We will carry her and she will never step on the ground." She was permitted to go and they carried her to the grove. Playing, she saw a baby porcupine in a tree and she wanted it. The girls said, "We will get it for you."

"No, let me get it myself," and she climbed to almost touch it, but it moved a little higher. She kept moving as the baby porcupine moved. She would almost get it, and it would move a bit higher. She was unaware, busy trying to catch the porcupine, that the tree was growing, carrying her higher and higher, until at last it pierced the sky into the Upper World. Here the porcupine took on his proper form as the Sun God who could transform to anything, human or sunlike.

He made her his wife, and after they were married and lived in a teepee a while, a boy was born to them, the Sun Boy. The Sun God would go out and hunt to bring in meat, as game also inhabited the Upper World. She often went out to pick wild berries for food, also wild vegetables and roots. She was warned not to go near a certain plant—we call it ai-chune.

It also grows here in our country. It is a very delicious plant and it has pretty blue flowers. It is about six or eight inches high and the roots form like a small turnip with a heavy cover of skin. You do not cook it. You dig it and peel it. It's snow-white and has a clean nice flavor. All Indians love it. They form ai-chune parties and go out where it grows, near rocks and in black soil, a few inches underground. They dig these plants with a sharp instrument, knife or small shovel. They are easy to get. After the season, late May and early June, the tops dry up and ai-chune remains under the ground. It is hard to locate then, but in the spring when they are in bloom, you can see them from a long distance. There are two varieties. One grows straight with a short stem and it is the original, but the other has a long stem over one root. The one you do not eat is called Gowo-ah-chune. Now we go back to our story.

Her husband warned her not to go near the plant that the buffaloes had eaten the top off of, not to try to dig it up, just to leave it alone. She always passed them up until one day her curiosity got the best of her. She began to think: I wonder why he does not want me to dig the ones that have the tops bitten off? So she came to one whose top was eaten off by buffaloes. As she dug it up, the whole block of dirt came out with the plant and left a hole like a window. She looked down and could see the world she used to live in.

At this time, she put the dirt back with the plant and went home. She began to wonder how to get back to the world where she used to live when a young girl. As her husband went buffalo hunting, she requested him each time to bring back a choice piece of meat, called Dain-kee, which means a tenderloin. It's from along both sides of the backbone. Inside of this meat was the sinew that the Kiowas used as cords to tie feathers on arrows. It is very stout cord; you can't break it with the hands. The Kiowas also used this cord for bow strings. They plaited it together in long cords.

As he brought the meat, she saved these cords and wove them into a long line. After a course of time she thought she had enough, so after he left to hunt, she went to where her stob was locating the place. She dropped the cord down into the hole until it reached the end. She thought she had enough to drop to earth by the cord rope made with buffalo sinew.

She waited until he went off again, and she took her Sun Boy and opened up the hole. She tied one end of the rope to the stake in the ground and she tied her Sun Boy and herself onto the other end, then began to drop down to earth. They got to the end of the rope, but it failed to touch the ground.

It left her and the Sun Boy dangling above the ground.

Her husband, the Sun God, came home from the hunt, and she and the Sun Boy were nowhere to be found. He went searching for them. Almost exhausted, he found where she had dug an ai-chune whose top had been eaten by a buffalo. Looking down, he saw his wife and boy dangling almost to the ground. He, being a God, could command the stones to obey. He talked to a very heavy stone and caused it to roll down the cord rope and to skip the boy but hit the woman. It killed the woman, but it didn't hurt the Sun Boy, as he was gifted with the power of the Sun God which he had inherited. He dropped to the ground and began to wander about.

The story goes on a long time about the Sun Boy, and the Old Lady Spider Woman, and how the Sun Boy becomes two. That's what the name Zai-day-tall-lee means, two half-boys or twin boys. It is a long story and we cannot give all the details, but the most important one is that this Zai-day-tall-lee is the beginning of the Audle-beawa-hyn, as the Kiowas call them. Sometimes in ceremonies they are called Tal-lope Kaws, meaning Grandmother on the man's side, mother to her grandson. It seems in referring to all the Ten Grandmothers, the Kiowa word Tal-lope Kaws means all of the grandmothers.

The late Jimmie Blue Jay kept them. My father was a great believer and worshipped them in the ceremony. They bless according to poles used in the sacred sweat house, which we call the Tau-tat-aiw. When you master the rituals, you are entitled to inherit one of them. A Grandmother was offered to him, but he didn't accept it. Later it was given to Old Man Emanah Blue Jay, Togamote. He also had the two original Zai-day-tall-lees.

The Adal-heah-ya is the eucharistic body of the Kiowa supernatural teacher, the Sun Boy, whose human mother gave birth to him in the Upper World. He came down to this earth and lived a supernatural life with the wonderful powers he possessed. These powers were divided into ten parts, all existing today, and they are worshipped as Indian Gods.

ALLEN QUETONE: Dr. Winkler, you mentioned several times that true folklore all over the world speaks in images that are alike in the mythology and legends of various nations and races. If residues of such a universal language still exist, could a story like the one just told be interpreted in a way that non-Indians can understand?

DR. FRANZ WINKLER: You know, of course, that it was Carl Jung who proved the existence of a universal language in myths, legends and certain dreams. But while I admire him very much for this discovery and many other reasons, I do not believe that his interpretation of what he called archetypal images is entirely satisfactory.

I am also a little reluctant to attempt an interpretation of the beautiful story which Mr. Quetone told us, for the following reasons. The pictures in such stories are supposed to speak directly to the heart and represent a reality greater than any intellectual abstraction. I believe that people like you whose hearts still fully respond to such stories may consider an attempt at interpretation unnecessary and somewhat detrimental in its effect. However, the younger generation, losing rapidly much of the intuitive perception you still have, may come to consider the stories that have shaped your life merely poetic residues of the past. Whenever this happens, the spiritual heritage of a nation dwindles. It may be, therefore, of some value to point out that, while profound truths can be best expressed in archetypal pictures, they *are* translatable into intellectual terms and so are by no means merely poetic forms. Accordingly, I shall try to interpret some of the pictures contained in the story without attempting to interpret the story as a whole.

As I have said before, myths, legends and true visions deal with the creative element of which outer events are only shadows and reflections. In most such intuitively attained experiences, male heroes represent the spiritual element in an

67

individual or a nation, with its reflection in thoughts and actions. The female figures represent the soul element and its expression in emotions. In your story, the princess who was so precious that her feet could not touch the bare ground represents, I believe, a rather characteristic soul quality in the red race. Correct me if I am wrong, but I have always felt that there is an element of unearthly poetry in the Indian soul, so fragile and vulnerable that it never seems to have descended into the material reality of down-to-earth life. In this quality may very well lie the strength and the weakness of the red man. It gives him awareness of a non-material reality and the strength to give up his life with equanimity when his existence on earth becomes deprived of dreams. But it also makes him weak, as the Indian has not brought down into civilization all of his best inherent potentialities.

Yet this quality, while delicate and unable to descend fully to earth, causes also a longing to experience pain and to develop through the experience of suffering. The pine tree with its needles, and the porcupine with his quills, attract the princess. However, instead of bringing her down to earth, they lift her even higher up into the embrace of the sun god, who represents the divine origin of the race. Once she is entirely removed from life on earth, a longing awakens in the princess to descend again into the daily consciousness of her people.

I believe that the plant that you call ai-chune, like other special kinds of food, strengthens the person's vitality and lust for life. The same effect was certainly caused by the red man's enjoyment of buffalo meat and the increasing use of its hide which made life on earth more desirable. It is, therefore, not surprising that ai-chune as well as ropes made of buffalo sinews played an essential part in bringing what is most sublime in the heart of Indians closer to earth again. As your story tells, the princess never reached the earth, but she succeeded in sending down an impulse responsible for the further development of the race. In virtually all religious and mythological tradition, it is the "son of divine origin," born to a nation or race, which expresses a new impulse in their evolution.

ALLEN QUETONE: Thank you, Dr. Winkler. Myths and legends have always been fascinating to the Indian. And they have been a source of strength and joy as well as comfort. What you say now may help non-Indians understand why these stories have always been so much a part of the Indian way of life.

CHAPTER V

INDIAN MYTHS AND LEGENDS

Mr. Kindle's brief demonstration of the Navajo pollen ceremony yesterday was one of the most moving moments of the conference. He had just concluded saying that all races live in a great house, with the sky as roof and the earth as floor and that prayers should be offered for all people to the ends of the earth. And then came his pollen demonstration, which graphically called to mind how pollen spreads far and wide and brings blessings to all people. At the end of his little ceremony he, quite unexpectedly, turned to Dr. Winkler and with a look of joy in his eyes, rubbed a little pollen on the Doctor's coat and then on his own. It was as though he were showing in a concrete way how an Indian could start a revival of religious awareness.

A spirit of good will and reverence filled this meeting.

Before going on to more Indian stories the reader may be interested in a few more facts about the storytellers.

Chief Joshua Wetsit went to Government school, but not beyond fifth grade. His father was a medicine man and he learned much from him. He also learned much taking parts in Wild West shows, starting with the trans-Mississippi Exposition in Omaha, Nebraska in 1898, where he played "Chief Geronimo" in sham battles with 500 horses and Indians from 200 tribes. He has met Presidents McKinley, Hoover and Truman. In 1939 he put on the Sacred Peace Pipe Ceremony in Canada for George VI and Queen Elizabeth of England. His main occupation has been that of rancher and farmer, but he has also held many leading positions in his tribe and has been active as a lobbyist in Congress.

Reverend Guy Quetone's visits to Washington have been mentioned, but not the fact that he has long been a Methodist minister, deacon and elder and has preached in more than a dozen missions and churches in Oklahoma. He has been President of his Intertribal Regional Conference, chairman and secretary of the Kiowa, Comanche and Apache Intertribal Business Committee, and has served as interpreter on reservations and in Washington. In his earlier years he was featured in two different movies.

Alexander Saluskin started out in an Indian boarding school at the age of 6 but was transferred to a one-room school house, and then his parents turned him over to an Indian relative who became his tutor, as he reported in one of the early sessions. Mr. Saluskin has been a real student all his life. He has done legal research as well as his study of Indian languages. He has attended Washington State University and other schools. An interpreter to his tribal council from 1918 to 1934, he became a member from 1944 to 1964 serving as secretary 4 years and chairman 8.

David Kindle is a man who is deeply religious and a real student of human nature. As he speaks no English, his activities have been restricted to his Navajo tribe. He is a firm but gentle man, handsome in his native Navajo costume, which was adorned with very beautiful Navajo jewelry. His manner was quiet and reserved. But he was unfailingly warm and friendly. His keen interest in the conference was evident, and his vivid stories were always very much to the point.

Our moderator, Allen Quetone, is a great-grandson of Chief Stumbling Bear, famous Kiowa chief and signer of the Medicine Lodge Treaty of 1867 which created the Kiowa, Comanche and Apache Reservation. He was born in Lawton, Oklahoma, and graduated from Fort Sill Indian School at Lawton. Before going to university, he enlisted in the U.S. Air

71

Force as an aerial gunner in 1944. In 1947 he helped organize the American Indian Veterans Association and served as Vice President. In 1958 he was named to a special commission called "Operation Bootstrap" to study economics and development techniques in Puerto Rico. He has served as moderator and consultant on panels at University of Oklahoma and University of New Mexico and also on radio programs. And now we return to Mr. Queton and the next discussion.

ALLEN QUETONE: There is one area on which we haven't elaborated; that is the stories and legends that teach our young people how to live a proper life according to the Indian way of life. Perhaps we should tell some legends or stories that are used to teach the young people the Indian moral standards. Our tribe, the Kiowas, have the Saindee stories. This man, Saindee, represents all things that are bad about man, the undesirable character traits, so there is a moral to each story.

JOSHUA WETSIT: The Sioux character like that is Ick-tow-bee. We don't tell them much any more. The stories were long to begin with, but now we condense them down.

ALFRED BOWMAN: We have a legend that runs this way. This is figuratively speaking. The coyote's a man of doubtful nature. He's either for good or he's for bad. He can play both sides of the coin. He and the Frog Spirit argued which one of them would be the lord of the rain, that is, the one to send down the rain to the earth and replenish the earth and nature. The arguments were as good on both sides, and they wanted to settle the question. Mr. Coyote's a fast runner. He says, "Let's race over it. Whoever wins the race will be the lord over the rain, over the moisture element of nature." Mr. Frog knows he doesn't have a chance, but he says, "Give me time to think this over. The challenge is all right, but give me time to think this over."

Mr. Frog consulted his frog neighbors, and they finally agree to help him. They worked out a relay where the first frog would make a hole in the ground after one leap and stay there. One leap, then there was another frog. So on, down the length of the track. Mr. Frog had accepted the challenge: "Certain day, we'll race over it. I want to be the lord of the rain, and Coyote wants to be the lord of the rain." So they settled down to a race.

The day of the race came and these frogs each leaped his distance, then buried himself in the ground. They started the race. Coyote thought he had everything all sewed up, but he's bothered with an object close to his ear and side, almost all the time the whole length of the race track. It so happens that when they started, the first frog leaped to the second frog and the second frog leaped next, so they were abreast all the time to the end of the race. Coyote was looking back. He thought he had it all, but he didn't.

Then they argued who really won the race. Frog said, "I did." Coyote said, "I did." There was no settlement, so they came to a compromise. "Let's split the authority. I'll have certain portion of control over this moisture and Frog will have certain portion." The rough rain, where there's lot of lightning, went to the Coyote; and the gentle rain, the absorbing kind, the Frog had that. That's the way the authority was split.

The idea is that things like that could be won by crookedness or cleverness. The winning part is all right, but there still might be an argument. The next thing is to compromise, and that is in a certain way beneficial to both parties.

DR. FRANZ WINKLER: Practically all the stories I have heard have their equivalent in middle European folklore. It is almost a surprise how similar they are. It shows, I believe, how the original wisdom is universal, because there's certainly no contact between those very old European stories and the very old Indian stories that you have recorded in the artistic, intuitive, imaginative language of folklore and myths.

A similar story exists in Europe. The birds, trying to decide who should be chief among them, agreed that he who

73

flies highest will be king. As expected, it is the eagle whose great wings lift him above all the others. But when at last he, too, has reached the limit of his strength, he hears a tiny voice calling down from the sky. Looking up in surprise, he sees a small bird hovering a few feet above him. The little bird had hidden in the eagle's plumage and taken to his wings only when the eagle's strength had been spent.

The birds appealed to the Great Spirit to put the weak little creature in his place. But the Lord denied their appeal and said, "He has deserved his victory. Let him be king among the birds." Thus it came about that to our day his descendants are called "Kinglets."

If we try to interpret this story which, like all true folklore, is an example of intuitive wisdom, we must realize that most such tales deal with subtle changes in consciousness. It originated probably in the Middle Ages, at the time when the ideals of chivalry had reached their peak. Individual strength and prowess no longer sufficed. A new psychological quality was emerging in human consciousness, a quality that, for better or worse, was to determine the future. It was man's growing ability to gain power by intellectual design. In the story just told, this emergent quality assumes a legitimate place in the world, not by opposing the great forces of the past but by making the limit of their scope a new point of departure.

For years I have studied the folklore, myths and legends of different peoples and am deeply impressed with the similarity among them. Of course it was Jung who first made this fact widely known. True folklore is the last residue of "the one language," the language of archetypal images that, according to the tradition of almost all cultures, once formed a bond between the various peoples and races all over the globe.

According to the Bible, strife broke out among the nations of the world when the one language was "confounded," and people's hearts could no longer understand one another. Even today, the healing effect of the one language can still be discerned in myth and legend. Their magic is lost on the modern intellectual, who rejects their message as untrue and cruel. The critics of true fairy tales fail to see that these stories do not refer to outer events but to occurrences within. The often harsh punishment meted out to the evil sorcerer or witch does not incite cruelty toward others; it exhorts the child to be merciless in fighting evil in his own soul, for the scoundrels in the story represent cruelty, greed or other qualities that a human being must learn to overcome.

If grownups do not spoil such stories by their own lack of understanding, children will accept them joyfully. For the unspoiled child still has some intuitive understanding for the one language, with its healing and harmonizing effect. We all have experienced how quick youth of today is to reject the abstract rules and moral exhortations of their elders. But the bedtime stories they have heard as children will retain a place in their hearts. Thus in legends and fairy tales moral standards may find their last and only stronghold, in the never-ending struggle between light and darkness.

GUY QUETONE: I will tell you about a Kiowa boy named Tau-kaw-tal-lee, meaning Antelope Boy. He was an orphan boy, and he lived with his grandma.

Grandma had made a buffalo horn-spoon for Antelope Boy. He had it on a string around his neck, so whenever he wanted it, he always had it. One time he needed his spoon and he didn't have it. He had lost it. Grandma said, "If you don't find it, I'm going to punish you." He couldn't find it, so Grandma had to punish him.

They just had a wigwam where they lived. They were a poor family; just he and Grandma lived together. Grandma sent him into the wigwam as punishment for losing the spoon. He laid down next to the stakes holding the wigwam, so he could get a little air. He cried himself to sleep and he had a vision: the Spirit gave him power to materialize game.

75

The Spirit showed him what he was supposed to do, the ritual and the song.

There was a great famine among the Kiowas, and the bands were called to get their medicine man to produce some food. No one could be found to produce food. Antelope Boy told his grandma, "Tell the chief I can produce all the antelopes they need, if they will only follow what I say." His grandma answered, "No. They will kill us if you do not produce. We are too poor to be looked up to for food of any kind." The boy told his grandma, "You remember when I lost the black buffalo spoon and you punished me? I laid crying in our wigwam and a Spirit visited me and endowed me with this power." And he sang to her his producing song.

He gave her the instructions to give to the others. Everybody was to get ropes to tie down the antelopes, no guns or arrows. Everybody was to walk out in a long line until they came around in a ring and joined hands. They were to pull up white sage and throw it into the ring. If they wanted a lot of game, they were to make a big circle and throw in lots of white sage.

The next day the people gathered to do what the Antelope Boy said. As they came together and joined hands, Antelope Boy took his pipe and went through his ceremony. He sang his song.

The antelopes began to appear and they kept them running around in the circle until they were exhausted and fell down so they could be tied and butchered.

Toward the middle of the day there appeared a large buck antelope. Running around in the ring, he sang a song through twice. The words of the song were, "It's not me that's going to die that I'm crying and mourning for. It's not me that's going to die but my children, my descendants that I'm crying for." He blew his breath and ran towards several men holding hands, and jumped over and got away. The people commenced to catch the antelopes, tie them up and butcher them. Everybody had plenty of meat, and Antelope

Boy had proved his power.

ALEX SALUSKIN: This is a story told about Spee'l-yai. The word "spee'l-yai" means copier or a person that is a braggart. If someone does anything, he's always better than that fellow. When he tells his story or attempts to express himself, he's better.

His relatives died, his father, mother and brothers. He was grieving over them and wondering why should people die and disappear from the earth, leave us in sorrow — and what is going to become of humanity if something isn't done about it. These things were his thoughts. The Sister Spirits heard him, and they said, "Brother Spee'l-yai, if you want to go up after your relatives and bring them back so they could live everlasting life down here, you have to have a strong will power and you have to be persistent. You have to have perseverance. If you have that kind of heart, we will tell you how you can get your relatives back."

"All right. Whenever you reach the place where you're going, the Great Spirit will make a bundle for you of all your relatives, whoever you want to bring back to earth. When you bring it back, no matter what happens, you must look forward and have a strong heart. Never get frightened. Do not look back."

"That's simple. I can do that." So given permission from the Sister Spirits to go, he left the earth and he reached up to the Great Spirit. Because of his communication with the Sister Spirits his coming was already known. The Great Spirit said to him, "All right, Spee'l-yai, I have your relatives all bundled up. There they are in a little pack." He was instructed to put it on his back, and he started down to earth with his pack.

The first day, it was fine. The second day, he got a little tired. The third day, he was quite tired. The last three days he had been hearing a remote noise, like someone was behind him. Of course he had been told not to look back, never to get frightened. He had his mind made up that he would always look forward and travel forward. The fourth day, he just had will power to drive himself. He still heard the noise, and he was near to losing his confidence by the first part of that day. On the fifth day, that noise was so tremendous, it sounded like it was right on top of him. He figured that this was the end of his life. He dropped that pack and started to look back. When he looked back, he saw his people going back.

The moral of that is, if you want to accomplish anything, once you make up your mind to do it, you'd better carry it out; never change your mind or get frightened. If it is necessary to give up your life for what you believe, you should do it. So Spee'l-yai failed to bring his relatives from the dead. From there on, since that day, we are to live here for a certain period of time, and then we die and our souls go some place.

DR. FRANZ WINKLER: One of the great ancient legends of the Greeks was about a person who later on also became the God of Music. He loved his wife so much he went to the Nether World, and with his music he succeeded in winning over the God of the Nether World and got his wife back. The only condition was not to look back. He just couldn't resist. He looked back and he lost her again. It's exactly the same.

SYLVESTER MOREY: They must have a common origin. They must have been inspired by some central core.

DR. FRANZ WINKLER: Legends like these could unite the whole world if it were understood that they represent a common language. Its loss was a tragedy. Revived, they may form a common bond between races and nations.

JOSHUA WETSIT: Ictowbee is a man who makes himself into everything. No matter what it is, he usually wins out. We also call him the Yellow Liar because he is champion at telling lies.

Ictowbee went to a big encampment where they were having ceremonial dances. Everybody was having a good time, but he criticized them. He said, "Those people dancing there, they're not eligible to be dancers. They never went to war. They never got a coup or did anything good for the people, and yet they're dancing in front of the chiefs and women. They're not qualified. We don't allow that kind of leadership around here."

That kind of broke them up and as they broke camp, two fellows took exception and said, "We just as well go on the war path now because we're not eligible to dance." One was a turtle and the other was a sturgeon. They started out together. They went down the river, and after a little while they took a look on the bank. There was a teepee by itself with a family living there. They said, "There's our enemy now. We will see what we can do."

There were several in the family there. One of them picked up the sturgeon, and two others were going to pick up the turtle, but the turtle kind of dodged. "What's the use of picking him up?" one said. "We'll just trample on him." They jumped on him with both feet and one knocked his heel out of joint and the other broke his ankle. They fell and couldn't move.

They don't know how to kill the fish because it had horns on each side and back. They already had a fire going with a big pot of boiling water. They tried to throw him into the water, but they fought and knocked over the pot. It spilled and burned the two who tried to cook the fish.

"What are we going to do with them? We can't kill them." One said, "We'll just throw them down the river there." They had come out of the river, but the turtle started to cry, "Oh, I hate to be in the water." The other one cried too. "That's the way you feel about it, then let's throw you in there," and they did.

Some time after that, at another encampment, these fellows came to the ceremony. "We're going to take part. We got our scalps now. We're eligible to dance." They had bows and arrows and the turtle painted himself red, here and there, with war paint. The other fellow did too. Here came

Ictowbee along. He made fun of them. "Look at these two fellows, what they're doing now. They're all touted up." He said, "Look, he's got paint too." They answered, "That's our enemies' blood."

"Enemy blood!" he said, and he just kind of pushed them away. The sturgeon started to sing his war song. He said, "The turtle killed two persons, and I killed the whole camp." So that outwitted Ictowbee. He got a kick out of it, but that was the encouragement that he gave. He reproached them to be warriors. He made fun. "If you don't, you're a woman."

That's the end of that. You can go to sleep on that.

ALEX SALUSKIN: That last word, "You can go to sleep on that," that was the conclusion of all these legends in our camp, meaning, "Tomorrow you'll have good sunshine, you must go to sleep now," concluding the stories.

SYLVESTER MOREY: Do you tell these legends on certain occasions?

JOSHUA WETSIT: You aren't supposed to be telling these legends in the daytime. That's a rule. These stories are handed down three-four-five nights, maybe a week. They could tell you that story for an hour, two hours; and as long as you keep saying, "Uh," you mean that you're listening. Every so often, "Uh." Soon as you quit saying it, he's going to stop. That's the end of it for that night.

ALLEN QUETONE: Children would always have to say that so the story-teller would know when they stopped saying "Uh" they're asleep. As long as they were saying it, they were listening to the story.

DAVID KINDLE: I would like to tell a legend here which is both meaningful and, I think, ties into the present policy where the Federal Government is combatting the proverty question.

In this morning's legend I told about the Sun God. The Sun God made preparation for the inhabitants of this earth. He killed all the monsters, everything that would prey on the people. When he thought he had got rid of all the monsters that would be deadly to the people, that would devour the people, he thought he had finished his role and he was coming back to his home on that little mesa that is the cradle of our origin. Then he met someone and asked him, "I thought I killed all the enemies of the people. Are you still alive, or where did I dodge you?" Then he found out this was Poverty.

"No, grandchild, I don't want to be killed," said Poverty. "If you kill me, then it will be the end of humanity, because you will have no knowledge of the needs, the necessity of one another, and the urge to do things for yourself and others. I should be here, and it will help you to develop compassion for one another. There will be need, there will be necessity, there will be the urgency to do things for yourself and for those around you because you are a human and you have certain needs. Your moccasins will wear away and there is a necessity that you got new moccasins. It develops your mind that you have to acquire and look for those things you need and others need. If you kill me, you will be like the rest of the animal world, without compassion for your fellow man and concern for yourself. You, as a human, should retain me. But I'm not the only one. There are four of us all in this category."

The first one that he meet, he didn't kill — he didn't kill Poverty. He didn't kill the need. He didn't kill the want. He saw that man needed poverty to be humble and to be concerned with the needs of others as well as himself.

He met another one — as the first one stated, there were four of them. He met the second person. The Sun God boy says, "I thought I killed all the monsters that would be killing the humanity on this earth, but I notice that you're still alive." The answer came that he didn't want to be killed because "I have a definite purpose to live and to stay with you." He found it was Hunger. "Because I must have a place in your life to bother your stomach. When your stomach

81

becomes empty, you will feel that you're hungry and you will think, develop your mind about how to get food. You will become industrious and stop being lazy. You will go out and look for game or into the fields to get the crop. I have a definite purpose to live with you people. Without me you will be lazy and couldn't develop the qualities of mind and strength you should have for this world."

So that's the second person he let go. Hunger was not killed. The Spirit of Hunger was not destroyed. It was left purposely to remain with us to make us work.

Then he went ahead and he met the third person. He asked him the same question. "I thought I had killed all the enemies of humanity. Are you still around here yet? How was it I missed you?" He found that it was Fatigue. Every night we should go to sleep. It's a must if we are not to forget the world of the spirit. We have to have the sleep to be in good health. "If you kill me," said Fatigue, "you will never rest. You have to have your sleep each night, to replenish both your physical and spiritual strength. Without sleep, man would forget the spirit and be aware of only the physical world. If you kill me, that will be the end. Your eyes will dry up. You won't get the necessary rest to continue your life."

So he didn't kill him. He let him abide with humanity. But there is an extreme to that thing, too. If you do nothing but sleep and sleep, you'll die of poverty. You'll be lazy and die of want. It is part of the life necessity to sleep, but if you continue to do nothing but sleep, you'll fall into the hands of hunger which forces you to work. He let Fatigue go because it was necessary that he be retained as a help to humanity.

He went on again and met the fourth person. He told him the same thing, "I thought I had killed all the enemies of humanity, and here you are. You're still alive." He found it was Body Lice. He wanted to kill him, but the Body Lice also has a purpose. Without lice, people wouldn't bother to keep clean. When people come together to comb each other's hair, it's kind of leisure period for them. Those periods, they'll be talking about something that happened with the community. It serves a purpose that they have the time to visit. Body Lice forces people to make an effort to keep clean and to be sociable.

So he wasn't killed, either. Body Lice he let go, to abide with humanity.

Four of those, as a group, were given freedom to operate in their sphere. By viewing this legend, we know that it definitely has a purpose. It is a problem — how to combat the needs in a person's life, how to think of others, what to wear, what to eat. Is he tired? Does he need that rest? Does he need that cleanliness? To my knowledge it is those things that are an aid to humans and force us to think, to act. I think it was well that they were spared; otherwise our efforts for the needs of the human race would have dried up.

ALLEN QUETONE: I would think this story is the Indian's explanation of a plan for man and the necessity of existing with his physical environment.

I heard a lot of these stories as I was growing up, but I never really knew their purpose. Looking back, I think my own character has been influenced by the early training and stories I heard as a child from my grandparents. The morals of these stories are strong, and they have a very effective influence on your character and personality.

After you have been away for, say, fifteen years and go back to the community or the reservation, the Indian life and Indian values and the communications you have with your own people automatically assume the Indian character or the Indian way of doing things. You leave the area and you start "going by the clock" again.

In our tribe, the philosophy and training that young people received stressed character traits which pointed to a goal of leadership. Only those persons who practiced and possessed all the good traits of character could become leaders. This, of course, involved the development of qualities such as courage, generosity and kindness.

Leadership of the tribe and the method of selection tie in with following through with the spiritual essence of Indian life. All of this training program was tied in with the spiritual beliefs of the tribe, the belief of the Higher Power, and the fact that certain strengths of character were attained because of this spiritual power.

I don't know exactly how a lot of this training was accomplished, but these gentlemen would know how this was achieved. I don't know if it would hold true today because of our constitutional democratic system of electing leaders; but in the old days (and I think this needs to be really publicized in the white world) the good leaders had to possess these qualities. The good leaders were the ones that held the real leadership of our tribes. The true democratic process of the Indian way in selecting their leaders was that they naturally moved toward the man who provided the type of leadership that was for the best interests and welfare of the tribe. As a result, it was a voluntary process, so that the best leaders had the biggest camp or the largest following, and of course the nucleus was always the family.

Even after they became leaders, if they violated any of the chieftain requirements in their executive functions of leadership, they could lose their standing. If there was a violation or if a chief didn't measure up, he would wake up some morning without any followers, except for his immediate family. This method is one of the things that served towards strengthening community relations and people relations.

ALEX SALUSKIN: From these legends and stories, the training was for honesty, aggressiveness and accumulation. If you have wealth, you are capable of providing for your family, as well as the old and the dependent people.

For example, when the Indians set their weirs across the Columbia River and its tributaries, they stopped all the fish for a certain period of time. After gathering the fish, they distributed them to every individual or individual camp,

depending on how many there were in each camp. Under the laws of the Yakimas, once the village had sufficient salmon, they didn't stay there and exterminate the fish just because they had the power to stop those fish from migrating up the streams. They took their weirs up and put them away and went about harvesting other native food. There is a legend in regard to that.

This fellow competed in athletics, and he imitated one of his superiors and falsified his credentials; so he was disqualified from the contest. It was the end of the season, and the bear was hibernating, the ground hog was hibernating, the ground squirrel was hibernating, and all had their provisions. He began to wonder: What have I got? He thought about his relative, the crane. He knew where the crane lived, so he thought, "I'm going over there and I can probably impose upon my relative."

He got to the door of the cavern, and he heard the crane singing his medicine song. He could hear the rhythm made by the yew wood which the crane had put notches in. He walked in and looked around. "My goodness, this place is just filled with food. There's food around the sides of the walls. There's food on the ceiling. There's my cousin all alone." He thought his cousin was going to stop pretty soon and he would notice him and show him hospitality. He waited for the invitation; but this crane would sing for a while, then he would pull off one of the dried fish and put it in his long beak, devour it and commence to sing again. Spee'l-yai thought, "He's going to get his fill pretty soon. He'll stop singing and he'll invite me to have some food." The crane didn't stop.

He was there four days. On the fifth day, he didn't get invited, the crane was still singing. So he figured, "As long as he's not paying any attention to me, I guess he doesn't notice me; so he won't miss anything." He started to pick up some of the food and devour it himself. When he reached out, his cousin and everything disappeared and it seemed like he regained his consciousness. He looked around. "This is a

85

barren place, a cold barren place." From there on his conscience told him: If you're going to be eating, you better get out and collect your own food.

So your cousin could be rich, but you can't depend on him. You better hustle for yourself.

In the same manner, we talk about the raccoon. There was an orphan boy, and his grandma was raising him. His grandma says, "Grandson, you better go down to the cache and get some acorns." He was hungry for acorns, so he ran down and filled up his little pouch. He started back and stumbled. The acorns spilled. No need to let them go to waste, so he ate all of those acorns. He went back again, picked up some more and put them in the pouch. He started out again. He thought, "That was pretty good. I slipped right hereabouts and I spilled those acorns. They tasted pretty good." So he actually made it a point to slip the second time and he again ate all those acorns.

He did that five times, and his grandma knew what he was doing. She went down there and caught him. Instead of putting the acorns into the pouch, he was really eating the cache. So grandma started to whip him and call him a name every time she hit him, from the nose right down to the end of the tail. That is why the raccoon has that mark clear down to his tail. She told him that hereafter you'll never be a human, you're going to be a raccoon. You'll go out there and hustle for your food. So don't be a raccoon.

GUY QUETONE: When a young man was growing up, he had to prove himself worthy to be a leader. He had to grow up ambitious, be a good rider, be courteous and kind to everyone, be brave and always willing to help and even die for another person if necessary to save his life.

In the first expedition he had to prove himself to have the strength and character required before he would be accepted. So at an early age, he went out with an expedition, a party of grown men. Sometimes they made camp maybe a few hundred miles from the main camp. They were going to

86

approach the enemy. If they thought he's too young, they would leave him with the other young men, to take care of the ponies and baggage that they have carried along.

Maybe he said he's able to go along and take care of himself. If they thought he might be able to, they told him what he had to go through, that he might be killed and nobody would look out or care for him. If he said, "I'll take the risk," he went out with the party.

There is a story of two young men who started for leadership. One of them was twelve years old and the other was fourteen. The boys went with a party into New Mexico and Colorado, along the eastern route, going to Mexico to steal horses. When they went into Mexico, the Mexican soldiers heard that they were in the community. They succeeded in hunting this expedition out and they had a battle, killing everyone except the two boys who got away in the dark while they were fighting. They were too young to know the way back home. They didn't know where the water holes were and they didn't have horses to go on. They might run into some enemies and get killed. The older boy said, "Let me be the leader and you follow my advice and maybe we'll get home."

Instead of taking the route that they came by, they took the western route, following the Rocky Mountains. Some Comanches were going to hunt Sioux Indians and they met them. This Comanche said, "You're too little to be out for yourself. If you go along with us and if we don't all get killed, we'll take you back home." So they went with the party.

The Comanches, instead of hunting the Sioux, changed to go horse stealing. They drifted into New Mexico and the boys were told to go out and bring in any horses they could find. They went out by themselves and brought in a herd to join the Comanches.

When they got home, the Comanches told the story about the boys out by themselves and getting such a big herd of horses. The boys gave the Comanche chief and other leaders horses out of their herd because they had horses to spare. The oldest one was selected as a young war leader because he had proved himself, that he was brave and ambitious and brought a herd of horses home, as any grown leader could.

The next party he went along and proved that he was an early riser and a good scout. He then had a little experience and he proved that he could be depended upon. Whenever they went on a war party, the first one that could give a coup, that went to his credit. When he got four coups he was recognized as promoted to a "Towyokee," a leader. After he proved himself to be a Towyokee, he could recruit a band and take them out because he knows the route, where the water holes are and which direction to find the enemy. Other leaders may join but they had to go under his orders.

On expedition, everybody gets up before sunlight, but this man oversleeps three or four times. Finally, the other men cut saplings about four or five feet long. While he sleeps, they put them under his bed and at the same time as they yell, everybody turns him over with the poles and he wakes up. That's a mark, that it is no good.

Another way, when cooking breakfast, they make a coveted dish, made from the inside of buffalo. The fellow that is training for leadership, while he sleeps too long, the one that's doing the cooking puts a little meat and a piece of rawhide inside and it's marked. They pass it around. When they come to that rawhide one, it is for the lazy fellow. Everybody is eating and he can't cut his meat off. Finally he bites hard and pulls out the rawhide. Everybody makes fun of him. That's the sign, he's not qualified to be a leader.

A person has to have all the traits, honesty, ambitious, kind-hearted, good horseman, to be selected as a leader.

Chief Dragonfly, the man with a long knife, Chief Mosquito, the young man with a fine voice, and Chief Frog who had a big bass voice, and others started off together. The river was high and overflowing, so when they're going across, Chief Moccasin floated away. When they got to the other side of the river, they had to mourn for him. Chief Frog with the deep bass voice mourned too loud and his voice split and he died. They went on several miles and came to a muddy creek. Chief Grasshopper got some mud on his foot. He tried to kick it off. Instead of kicking the mud off, the whole of his leg came off, so they had to mourn him.

They went on and after a while they came to enemy territory. Chief Mosquito was sent out to spy the country. In the night he went around and sang in the chief's ear to see if he was deep enough asleep. While he's singing, the chief heard his voice, put his hand up and killed him. When he didn't come back, Chief Dragonfly went over and found that the chief had killed Chief Mosquito. Chief Dragonfly with the long knife cut the chief's head off. He didn't have time to scalp him, so he took the whole head. They all woke up and commenced to trailing him. He went back to headquarters where Chief Snapping Turtle was. Chief Snapping Turtle took the head and put it under his arm and coiled up in his shell. They killed Dragonfly, but they couldn't kill Chief Snapping Turtle. They shot arrows at him and the arrows slipped on top of his hide and killed another one over there. Every time another one was killed, Chief Snapping Turtle said, "There goes another enemy."

"What are we going to do? We can't kill him by shooting at him. Let's burn him up." They piled wood and Chief Snapping Turtle thought he would crawl under the wood. "He hides in the wood. He likes fire. We can't burn him. See him crawl under there before we burn it. Throw him in the river and drown him." Chief Snapping Turtle cried like he was afraid of water. "He's afraid of water — throw him in there." So they threw him in the water and he dived under to the other side. From there he took the head, waved it, and went home victorous.

DR. FRANZ WINKLER: Your stories are beautiful examples of

folklore at its best. If they were forgotten, humanity would be deprived of a treasure. But since they are being discussed in context with our conversation on education, certain questions as to their part in pedagogy might arise. One of them is: How can the often warlike message of these stories be reconciled with your frequently expressed statement that education ought to strengthen love for peace in youth?

Personally, I find no contradiction here, since qualities like peacefulness, compassion, love for freedom, must precede their manifestations in outer life. Attempts by utopians made time and again to put enforcement of peace, justice and freedom ahead of educational effort to improve human nature, have often led to disaster. One of the many examples was the bloodshed following the French Revolution. Today, our civilization has brought forth the kind of weapons and warfare which can serve no imaginable constructive purpose, except of course in defense against aggression. However, there have been many occasions in world history when acts of war were compatible with an inner quality of peacefulness.

To understand history, we must try to discern the great differences which existed in the consciousness of a specific era and of the nations living in it. Naturally, human nature is such that people almost never live up to their ideals. Yet, even if imperfect, those ideals have given mankind invaluable gifts. The ancient Greeks give humanity the ideals of freedom, democracy and true harmony. In real life they kept slaves, practiced tyranny and often persecuted their greatest artists. Nevertheless, their ideals survived. The Romans gave man the concept of law and justice, in spite of their well known acts of injustice in actual life.

The Indians have given to the world ideals which have inspired the youth of two continents. They fought many wars and did many things contrary to their own ideals. Yet the violent history of Indian culture was not totally incompatible with peacefulness as expressed in your legends.

90

The brave is supposed never to lose his equanimity. In war parties, morale was usually maintained by voluntary obedience which seldom required the military discipline necessary in other armies. As far as I know, there existed little crime within the tribal society. Property was not individually held and the needy almost never denied a fair share in the resources of the tribe.

I believe that this idea of Indian warlike peacefulness ended only with the coming of the white man, when dislocations disrupted the red man's economy and brought hunger and want to the tribes. Then raiding parties were sent out to obtain food and cattle. The introduction of alcohol with its addictive properties undermined the Indian's ability to control his lower instincts, with the consequent loss of self-respect. The whole pattern of Indian warfare deteriorated and assumed a character entirely foreign to the original ideal of Indian chivalry. Greed, too, came into existence, chiefly with the introduction of three highly coveted possessions: the horse, the gun and fire water.

Yet manifestations of human frailty shared by the white and red man alike should not distract teachers of history from recognizing the invaluable gifts the white man received from the Indians. These gifts are not easy to define but they are implied in many of your stories. If I understand the Indian genius at all — and please correct me, if I don't — I would describe his legacy as follows.

The ideal of the North American Indian was to build a society in which man was the older brother but not the oppressor of his fellow creatures. He, therefore, had no desire to supplant nature by sprawling cities and a complex technological civilization. His purpose in life was not to exploit nature without but to become master of nature within. This mastery consisted of an ability to remain inwardly peaceful even under provocation and to fortify body and soul against cold, heat, hunger and pain. The true victor in this peaceful battle of life was the man who could face death even in its worst and most painful form. While the Indian usually loved life, he was prepared to prove his mettle if and when destiny put him to the supreme test.

Conflicts among Indian tribes had, therefore, a meaning different from wars fought among white men. The Indian of old was singularly free of greed. The main objectives of his fights were not the acquisition of property; nor did he want to acquire land which, according to Indian concepts, could not be owned. War, in theory at least, had the objective of testing a man's ability to rise above the natural fear of pain and death. It was a kind of sacred game in which the warrior offered himself to the Great Spirit for the supreme test of manhood. The victor who put his enemy to death merely did to his opponent what he himself was ready to suffer, should fate decide to put him to the ordeal. Consequently, the prisoner whose spirit rose above fear and pain was considered the true victor in the battle of life.

CHAPTER VI

APACHE RITUALS

In the last chapter the Indian Elders entertained and enlightened us with the telling of a few great Indian legends. In these legends we felt the wisdom that had been handed down through word of mouth from peoples of bygone ages who were close to the fundamental source of all wisdom — a source from which modern man has been all but cut off.

Dr. Emil Bock explained the origin of myths in his *The Apocalypse of St. John:*

"At the beginning of time, men were able to perceive supersensible beings in the realms of nature. All ancient mythology issued from these gradually fading, dream-interwoven visions of divine beings in the starry heavens and the earthly nature. After a final extinction of the old clairvoyance, an extinction essential for the development of a waking day-mind and the experience of freedom, an interval of intellectualism had to come which considered itself superior to mythology as being synonymous with superstition."*

Dr. Bock helps one to understand where the flashes of wisdom came from which are buried in the beautiful Indian

The Apocalypse of St. John by Emil Bock, published by Christian Community Press, London, 1957

stories — wisdom that is still to be found there unless the originals have been altered.

These tales need more telling — especially to young Americans, as they are the stories that are truly American and can teach young people to understand what life is really all about.

Consider David Kindle's story of the Sun Boy and the four Monsters that were spared because man needs to be harassed by such monsters — by poverty, for example.

A revival of the telling of such myths and legends will be necessary if we are ever to see the revival of morality that educators all hope for but do not know how to manage. The morality in these stories comes to the child in pictures that he can absorb and enjoy. Sermons, admonitions, and rational argument, we must admit, he either does not hear, or simply rejects out of an instinctive but well-founded antipathy for the merely intellectual.

During the course of the conference four distinguished Indians from out of town joined the discussions for as much time as they could spare from their other business. These men were Mr. Clarence Wesley (San Carlos Apache), Mr. Francis McKinley (Ute) Mr. Sidney Carney, (Seneca) and Mr. Forrest Gerard (Blackfeet). They all took a part in the activities, but only Mr. Wesley's conversations were recorded. The other gentlemen were only there for unrecorded sessions.

But now for a report on the meeting with Mr. Clarence Wesley.

ALLEN QUETONE: This session will be a discussion with comments on views concerning Indian traditions, customs, rituals and values by Mr. Clarence Wesley, a member of the Coyotero Band of Apache on the San Carlos Reservation who has had a varied background in Indian affairs. He has been Chairman of the Tribal Council of the San Carlos Tribe and also President of the National Congress of American Indians. He is now employed with the Bureau of Indian Affairs.

DR. FRANZ WINKLER: Indian culture has been capable of

94

inspiring young people all over the world, even though it is being carried by such a relatively small group. It is a little like the ancient Greek culture, which in its blossoming period hardly lasted more than eighty years, yet has inspired the world up to our days. There is something very similar in the Indian culture because all young people have taken inspiration from it. My impression is that the Indians at their period of greatness educated their children in an entirely different form from the way we do today. They not only imparted information, trained the children in skills, but they developed intuitive, creative faculties as well. Could you comment on this, please?

CLARENCE WESLEY: It is stated that we are educating our young people in such a way that perhaps our young Indians don't know about their own cultural values. There is too much emphasis on having the Indians adopt the dominant culture, and the problem we are faced with today is, "How are we going to revive some of the Indian culture that has already disappeared." Some of our own cultural values are fast disappearing on the San Carlos Apache Reservation. We had games, stories, ceremonial dances, that were very meaningful in the days of our older people. Today, in this process of education, a lot of these old ways are fast disappearing.

It is our right to get our Indian youth educated into professional men. At the same time, they should remember to keep the Indian identity. The Hopi Indians are keeping their ways, but at the same time, there are educated Indians on their reservation. There are teachers, nurses, lawyers and businessmen. There are a lot of capable Indians on the reservation. They have their own tribal council, and plans should initiate from the reservation level. So many times the Indians have been told: This is best for you and you should follow.

DR. FRANZ WINKLER: Education to me is partly intellectual. In the instance of the Hopi, there is training for skills and

95

professional training; that's intellectual training, which the present civilization can give. Then you spoke of songs and dances and other beautiful traditional habits, which in my opinion comprise the training of the intuitive faculties that keep the people together. These ceremonies and dances are actually training the intuitive creative faculties of the people who do them. I believe this was understood in the ancient or older Indian training, education. When the children were exposed to those habits, followed those dances, something changed and developed and grew in them that cannot grow from intellectual information. This is exactly what I have in mind.

Today we are training intellect in our white schools, and letting the inner self, the inner man, die. The result is all the futility, alcoholism and drug addiction, because the human being cannot live as if he were purely an intellectual animal. I believe we all agree that some divine spark in him has to be trained, brought out in artistic ritual and cultural exercises; and the redevelopment of those beautiful traditions is more than preventing culture from dying — it also could be the beginning of a new intuitive training of human beings, not just among Indians. The Indians could really show a way in which the civilization can be saved.

ALLEN QUETONE: Mr. Wesley, can you explain more about the customs that the Apache Tribe practiced to teach the young people as they entered the various stages of life, as the Indians knew it?

CLARENCE WESLEY: There is a ceremony where the tribe, or a particular family, celebrates the puberty of a girl, to honor this girl when she comes of age. The family gets another family involved, which is something like godparents. They bless this girl through this ceremony. There is exchange of food and gifts, sometimes even stock.

The girl dances two nights and two days; that is to build her up and give her strength. The ceremony is asking for blessing from the sky, from the sun, from the moon, from the stars. It is customary, not only with this particular dance, but in other ceremonials, to sing religious songs. There are a lot of songs that the Apache can sing: Bear Song, Deer Song, Coyote Song. It is all done in a sacred way.

From three to six months later, whenever the family involved and the parents of the girl feel like it, they again exchange food. They prepare all kinds of food and take it to their houses, even a beef, maybe two beeves. It is expensive in a way, but there is a purpose. It develops a good relationship between the two families.

JOSHUA WETSIT: The Assiniboine custom is similar to that. We celebrate when a girl reaches a certain age. They put up a teepee and bring the food, and their friends and relatives are invited to the ceremony.

The relationship you mentioned is very similar to our marriage ceremony; a great relationship is created there. The parents of each of the people, the woman and the man, come together. You are not buying a woman, but you give to each other as an honor.

ALFRED BOWMAN: Giving away gifts was not understood as the handouts of today. The ceremony when the girl goes into womanhood, giving the gifts, is one of the main ways the Indians teach to be kind to their fellow man. That is why they give anything they can or have. They instill in this young lady that she should be kind to all fellow men.

CLARENCE WESLEY: Another dance performed at this ceremonial is known as Devil Dance or Clown Dance or Mountain Spirit Dance. They perform over this girl for one night and the next day until noon. It's painting of the girl. Each Clown Dancer paints the girl with something like a limestone that's ground. It's been used for many years. Then at the end of the ceremony, the Clown Dancers go around in a big circle and throw this white powder all over the people that gather there. It's to bring blessing to the people, too.

ALLEN QUETONE: You have been exposed, not only through actual experience, but from what you have been told by your

97

parents and grandparents, to how some of these customs, rituals and ceremonials were taught. Some person within the tribe or family had a responsibility to do this, from the educational standpoint of what the young people needed to know, whether it was for hunting or for the girls, how to sew the tents or clothing or how to make food. A tribe still practices somewhat these methods of teaching young people how to do these practical things, as well as some of the cultural and social family things that they need to know. Speaking from my own experience, a lot of this training just happens as a matter of course or at appropriate moments without any formal training period, but then there is a formal training time for young people.

CLARENCE WESLEY: When I was a youngster, there were a lot of us in the same clan. There was in each clan a headman, equivalent to a chief. My grandfather was considered a chief, and his son's children and his daughter's children and all the other children of the clan would get together in the evening and Grandfather used to tell us a lot of things in the way of these religious practices. We would roast corn over coals and our grandfather would tell us these stories and songs. He gave us advice on how to be an upright individual, not to be lazy, to do things for yourself; and in that way you feel proud that you have brought yourself up, instead of going to the neighbor to ask for something to eat or some clothing to wear. He said you have to do things for yourself, and of course in those days we had no jobs. We went out and picked up what nature had produced for us. This is more honorable than to ask for a handout.

ALLEN QUETONE: This was the teaching of which character traits were good and which were bad. And there were songs with words that have a moral to them. Also, the legends: Each had a moral in it of what not to do, and the character represented the bad side of man. This is one method of teaching, and I was wondering if the Apaches had any legends or stories that brought out these things to the people.

CLARENCE WESLEY: These stories and legends meant something as told by the Indian, by the old-timers.

DR. FRANZ WINKLER: That's what we hope possibly still to preserve, but when you said that every legend, every story had a moral — why is it that if you simply said the same moral in so many words, it wouldn't work? It would have the opposite effect. There is nothing hated more by young people today than moralizing, ordinary intellectual moralizing, giving them good reasons why not to do this or to do that. This is what young people hate most, even if you warn them about something that will do them harm. It doesn't have any effect to say: Don't take LSD because it harms you. In those Indian stories and legends there is another element, which brings the moral message direct into the heart. You cannot get a moral message through the brain. You have to get it through the heart. This is what makes what I call intuitive training. It has to be enclosed in a different medium that is traditional, ceremonial.

I would like to formulate as clearly as possible for the sake of white Americans who are used to thinking in abstract terms the reasons for your resentment of charity. It is not, I believe, false pride — the country owes you a great deal — but because you feel that it does not come from an understanding heart. The ceremonies which in Indian custom must accompany the exchange of gifts take the sting out of charity by lifting it to a higher level of true humanity. On this level, the giver becomes the recipient of a special grace.

It was much the same in the older form of Christmas. Christmas is entirely a matter of gifts, and every child naturally wants something — that's human nature. But giving without ceremony, as is done now, makes the children morally worse after each Christmas. There is always disappointment about the gifts, because what children are really looking for is a ceremonial connected with the gift, so that the gift becomes not only physical property but an inner possession as well, which then leads receivers, too, to be generous.

Modern society has all but forgotten the qualitative aspect of giving and receiving gifts. True joy does not come from material objects but from the mood in which they are given and received. Children especially cannot find joy in receiving a gift, particularly the gift of knowledge, unless it is given in a way which will open their hearts as well as their minds. Maybe one reason Indians reject our school system is its disregard of the intuitive and ceremonial. For information is meaningless to a child unless it is part of a ceremony or story that stirs his sense of wonder.

CLARENCE WESLEY: This generosity is not one man's doing. It's a *group* of people who feel they should have this kind of ceremony for the girl. It goes with the meaning of the ceremony.

DR. FRANZ WINKLER: In other words, according to Indian ideals, education must be accompanied by ceremony. You do not educate a person by intellect or information alone. You need both. You need information and you need the ceremony that educates the inner man.

CLARENCE WESLEY: To maintain these ceremonies as education, there is simply the elder passing on to the youngster. That is, on the reservation they try to pass it on. The sad thing is, there's nothing written on it.

DR. FRANZ WINKLER: Could not then the tribe keep up as much as possible the ceremonial part? While teachers from outside could give the professional training (not that Indians could not do it themselves, but as long as there are not enough Indian teachers), Indian teachers, to the best of their ability, could educate the young in the ceremonies, giving the moral and artistic-creative elements — a combination of the two.

CLARENCE WESLEY: I would like to go along with that, yes; but there is another influence on the reservation, like some churches. One of the things they're saying is, "Forget your Indian ways, forget everything," and even, "Forget your language. You have to speak *English* so you can understand what the preacher is talking about, so you are able to read the Bible." A lot of the Indians don't go to the ceremonies any more. I have two aunts that tried the church. They had limited education and they were strong for a while, but they found out that they wanted to remain Indian, so they quit the church.

DR. FRANZ WINKLER: Don't you believe that maybe mistakes have been made, in that the beautiful traditions of the Indians have been kept perhaps immobile for too long? They were so beautiful that they were preserved practically as they were before the white man came, and they could not develop or progress further according to their own nature. This might be the reason the Indian tribes could no longer understand each other, became hostile to one another, because everyone became static in his own way and this prevented further developing.

The tradition that is beautiful should follow its own rules of life. Everything moves, everything in it transforms; and maybe this was not sufficiently done. If it is still in the heart of people like you, it can be reborn, even if the memory of the exact rituals is lost. And the danger of such a loss is very real. There is so much in Europe that was destroyed by wars and revolutions. And still some of its beauty could be renewed by determined efforts. I hope that the Indians will not abandon their heritage of beauty but revive it in a form appropriate to their time.

CLARENCE WESLEY: We all know that the Bureau of Indian Affairs and educators tell the Indian people, the tribal council, that the best way to achieve results is by getting the Indians "educated," teaching them to speak English when they're four years old, and that the public school is the answer. Like you say, all this is in strong opposition to this inner self and though we may try to teach our young in the ceremony, I don't think we'll get anywhere. There's so much emphasis on getting the Indians to be white men. That's why I'm saying we're losing the battle, and we'll continue to lose it.

I did a lot of tape recording of the Indian songs and stories, but like I say, a lot of our people are being told that learning the white man's ways is the best. I want my kids to be Indian. I told my kids, if you're going to be in Clarence Wesley's house, you got to talk Apache.

SYLVESTER MOREY: Is this what you have in mind? What you're saying is that there's a great deal for Indian children in white education and in white schools, but at the same time an interest in the basic Indian truths should be maintained? Indian parents want this for their children; they also want it for themselves. You don't want to eliminate white education entirely, but you do wish to turn things backwards as far as Indian culture is concerned and make it flourish once more. For from your festivals, your dances, and your legends children learn both morality and joy in life.

ALLEN QUETONE: This is something that you learn from the time you get up in the morning until you go to sleep at night. This is one reason why boarding schools are very bad for the young Indian people; they take these young students away from their homes to where there is no Indian culture involved in the teaching. If the parents were given more opportunity for guidance, they could instil some of the traditional things of the Indian culture. The counselor cannot do this. It has to come from the tribe, the family, parents, even from brothers and sisters, and the environment.

DR. FRANZ WINKLER: Education and philosophy are influenced today by the assumption that exposure to one single school system can unite the most different kinds of individuals in a kind of happy brotherhood. This concept has led the United States to spend vast amounts of money and energy on *unifying* education within and even beyond its borders. The general idea is that a minority brought up differently from the majority may form a hostile foreign body in society, while people brought up in the same way will eventually form one big happy family the world over. This is a generous and noble American theory and would justify any effort and sacrifice, were it not so utterly wrong.

Man's individuality is such that he detests seeing himself reflected over and over again in millions of others. Deep in his heart every human being longs to be unique, and demands help of the educational system in achieving his own particular possibility. Naturally, it is one of the most important duties of the educator to purge that legitimate feeling of uniqueness from unjustified conceit. Since no human being can be wholly perfect, children must be taught to look for perfection in the sum of diverse abilities as these exist in the world-wide fabric of the various races, nations and individuals.

Two extremist views seem to have spoiled, time and again, man's hope for happiness and peace. One is the dreary concept of "sameness," the idea that all men are alike, which would turn humanity into a great flock of sheep. The other is the arrogant idea of racial predominance, that some peoples are "better" than others, which would reduce mankind to a collection of hostile groups, forever fighting and destroying one another to prove an imagined superiority.

Actually, we can never hope to create a better world unless we take our clues from nature itself. Nations and races represent the vital organs of the body of mankind. Each of these organs is unique in its task and potentialities. All need one another for health and even survival. In the physical body, if you try to force a lung cell to behave like a cell of the heart, disaster will result.

Naturally, like all comparisons, this one too is inadequate. Our physical body does have organs of lesser importance, but the races and cultures constituting the body of mankind are all equally important. They become decadent and dispensable only when one of them either forsakes its particular mission in history, because it is imitating others, or else considers its mission superior to that of others. Most of the great tragedies in history can be traced to the elimination of one single national or racial unit. Spain, once the richest and most powerful nation of the world, succumbed to centuries of decline when she eradicated the remnants of Arabic and Jewish culture.

Thus I am personally convinced that the future of this country is inextricably bound to the survival of the Indian culture. Such a survival would require a tremendous effort on the part of the Indians themselves, since it cannot be brought about either by renewing the past or by forgetting that past altogether. It can be brought about only by seeking out the subterranean flow of Indian culture and raising it to the surface, not at the place where it once was, but at the spot where it now flows in the hidden reaches of the Indian soul.

To assure such a survival, you who still know the past must become teachers, not only at the elementary level, but also at institutes of advanced learning. Commissioner Bennett supported this conference warmly, partly because long before Mr. Morey and I met him, he had visualized colleges in which young Indians would receive first class modern education while simultaneously being guided by Indian leaders of the old stock. He understands so well the vital need for Indians to be educated in intuitive wisdom that he suggested that some of the guiding spirits of such academies may have to be taken from Indians who do not speak English; for only such people may still have access to the unspoiled wellsprings of Indian culture.

I fully agree with Mr. Wesley. All these dreams, which might not only restore happiness and greatness to the red man, but also save white America, will never come true unless one condition is fulfilled: Indian children must be brought up among Indian elders. Unless this is done, their hearts may be irreversibly closed to intuitive wisdom long before they reach the age of free choice in maturity.

CHAPTER VII

SUMMING UP

Here are the summing-up statements from the taped reports of the final sessions. What the tapes do not convey are the bright native costumes worn by several of the Indians at the final meeting.

The Denver Post had a staff writer and a photographer meet with the group at noon that day, and so the Indians had dressed for the occasion.

Several of the photographs taken by the newspaper photographer appear in this publication. The story of the meeting, written by Robert W. Fenwich, covered the top half of the first page of the Feature Section of the Sunday Denver *Post* of June 10, 1968.

Mr. Fenwich's heading read "Indians Hold Powwow on White Man's Ills" and his lead paragraph read "In an extraordinary change of traditional field positions, the American Indian was asked to Denver last week to ride to the rescue of the beleaguered white man."

Mr. Ben Black Elk's photo, alone, occupied a full quarter page in the *Post*. As a matter of fact Ben Black Elk is one of the most photographed men in America, as many visitors to the Black Hills of South Dakota know. In Denver, women followed him through the Hyatt House to get his photo and even invaded the meeting room to aim their cameras. Mr. Black Elk has a face that many people seem to think is "typically Indian." And yet,

105

in examining the faces of the other Indian Elders shown in the photos in this book, we see that each is distinctly Indian, though each is very different from the other.

Unfortunately, Chief Joshua Wetsit had to leave early the final morning, due to illness in his family. He had brought his Assiniboine tribal dress with him, and he was much missed in the photographs. The chief had also brought Andrew Jackson's sword with him — the sword that President Jackson had given his great grandfather. It had been on display in the meeting room and it was planned to have the chief show it off for the press.

A note must be added here about the contributions Mr. Alfred Bowman (Navajo) made to the Conference. Mr. Bowman came as interpreter for Mr. David Kindle. It is obvious that Mr. Bowman has often served as interpreter for Navajo leaders. He handled this assignment ably and, in addition, added many ideas and thoughts of his own to the discussion. He is considerably younger than Mr. Kindle, and is a fine, strong, alert Navajo, friendly and helpful. He was a credit to his tribe throughout our Conference.

The final sessions were cordial ones, as much good will had been generated between the Indians and the whites and also between the Indians of different tribes, some of whom had met here for the first time. The unusual discussions had brought the group closely together, so that more than information had been exchanged.

And now the final discussion.

ALLEN QUETONE: Dr. Winkler is to begin the summarization of our project.

DR. FRANZ WINKLER: The United States today is clearly at a crossroads. In their brief history, the American people have built the strongest, richest and most generous country in the world. Yet the use of drugs, racial strife, crime and violence, are reaching epidemic proportions. In other words, our civilization is one-sided; blessed by an abundance of intellectual abilities and technological skills, it is sadly lacking in an intuitive grasp of qualitative values such as the pursuit of true happiness through love of man and nature, through philosophical contemplation, and through religious experience. The Indian people, on the other hand, while they have not succeeded in building a strong, down-to-earth civilization, are endowed with intuitive faculties that may restore to American culture the inner strength it so badly needs in this crucial era.

History itself demands a true reconciliation between the two cultures, for the reason that a conquering civilization has seldom, if ever, flourished without receiving strength from the forces already existent in the conquered country. In America these forces have been weakened by suppression and neglect of the Indian, but in my opinion are still alive and full of promise.

The path toward a true living together of the red and white civilizations for mutual benefits must start with recognition of their differences rather than with any attempt to reshape Indians in the Image of White Americans. While it is the task of our government to provide Indian leaders with every possible opportunity to rebuild their own culture, it is up to the Indians themselves to bring what is so great in their heritage into a form appropriate to 20th century conditions. Since the wheel of history cannot be turned back, a restoration of Indian culture will have to be thoroughly modern, without, however, accepting the blatant errors and the pseudoscientific materialism of modern America and Europe.

Maybe this task could be approached by forming a school of higher learning, a true academy staffed with the spiritual leaders of the various tribes. These leaders, preferably chosen from men still deeply rooted in pure Indian thought-life, ought to formulate methods of physical and philosophical education to retrain the still existing intuitive faculties among their youth. Naturally, white students willing to participate should be included in such a program. College-educated Indian and white teachers* should be gradually included so as to create a faculty capable of educating their pupils to become well-balanced human beings.

What makes an individual modern in the true sense of the word is the educational effort to establish a balance between his intuitive and his intellectual faculties and to coordinate and synthesize both through the clear light of reason. It is the white man's tragic error to credit matter and energy with a reality superior to the reality of the invisible world of the soul. This error leads to a robot consciousness, a consciousness permitting man to conquer the world while losing himself.

The unrest among white students stems chiefly from the fact that white schools teach their pupils knowledge and skills but do not expand the core of the personality to the point where the student can *comprehend* what he learns. For comprehension is not the result of intellectual training alone but requires a balance between intellect and intuition. This was recognized in the academies of Greece, which, for example, taught the medical student man's relationships to the cosmos, and further trained his intuition through philosophical meditation and through creative art, before introducing him to anatomy and other disciplines of a purely intellectual and scientific nature.

Mr. Morey and I have been deeply impressed with the intuitive wisdom revealed in your attitude and in the beautiful stories you have told. These stories speak of man's eternal home, of his true nature, and contain a gentle strength that can fortify children for the trials of life. Yet they will survive only if they are accepted by the probing minds of a new generation. For young people are bound to

---

*The Waldorf Institute for Liberal Education at Adelphi University has these concepts in mind in training college graduates to become teachers. Up to now no Indians have taken the Institute's courses, but it is hoped that some will enroll in the not too distant future. Dr. Winkler, who is a trustee of Adelphi University, is much interested in the work of the Waldorf Institute.

108

ask: How can our parents' stories of creation and evolution be reconciled with the teachings of modern science? The answer, although simple, is surprisingly seldom given, for man and his world have a two-fold, not a one-fold history. One aspect deals with the deeds of the Creator, as told in the Bible and in all sacred traditions. The other refers to the outer manifestations and tangible results of divine action. The latter is expressed in Darwin's evolutionary theory, and the ensuing scientific world concept as taught in our schools.

Let me conclude my summary by expressing once more my heartfelt gratitude for the opportunity of meeting you. This was for me one of the rare occasions when a cherished dream, carried over from childhood, was for once verified by an experience in real life.

ALEX SALUSKIN: I'm a strong believer in Indian ceremonies. I've attended many Indian ceremonies and I'm a participant of the several we hold now at our encampment at White Swan.

We still hold the Peace Pipe Ceremony with a company of soldiers of the United States Army during the Flag Day Review. The Pacific Coast Sixth Army recognizes this day with the Yakima Nation, and they very generously try to carry out the treaty made when the Indians laid their guns down. From that day on, our peace pipe ceremony leader brings the peace pipe. After somebody lights it for him, he stands up to the east, to the north, to the west and to the south, indicating the four natural elements of the universe. Then he sits down and passes the pipe in the circle. Everybody that's in assembly gets the smoke out of that peace pipe. When that's completed, we have again perpetuated our agreement between the Caucasian race and the Indian Nation.

The Indians realize the full benefit of what we were discussing — and want to perpetuate this for the coming generations in modern life. We are proud of our old people, but we have to sharpen up the weapons for our young people. How are they going to meet the future situation and still be proud with their ethnic heritage? The purpose of our meeting here was to try to re-evaluate the Indians' part, with the anticipation of using the same cultural values in the future and trying to bring them to the present and future generations, so that our neighbor, the Caucasian race, would adopt some of them in order that there may be better understanding of all cultural and ethnic groups in this country.

I certainly want to express my appreciation for the Navajo representatives here, and especially Mr. Kindle. I think he was a great inspiration to this meeting, and of course Mr. Black Elk brings his philosophy, and Mr. Quetone, I think, is an outstanding person. Probably these gentlemen are fine examples of all these tribes that are represented here — and we have just commenced to understand the purpose of this gathering by the time we're adjourned!

BEN BLACK ELK: I'm very grateful to be here. Although we're different tribes, we have the same idea — to uphold our traditions as Indians, regardless of where we live. We hope our Indians will strive to retain their culture, will be proud they're Indians. As we say, we didn't dream these things, we had them in reality. Let's have all that come back again in a different way, a modern way.

GUY QUETONE: The emblem the Spirit gave to American Indians to recognize Him by is nature. You go out in the mountains where no man has gone. You are alone with the Spirit, and the Spirit is guiding you to show you His presence, when you are looking at the heavens, the sky, the clouds and the mountains, the trees, the rocks or the water. You can feel His presence. That's when the Indian takes this sacred pipe, smokes it, and offers thanks for the blessings and guiding and perpetuation in his life.

I want to thank the people that promoted this project. We know that it's putting new blood in the Indian way of life. Everybody wants to change the Indian's nature, but regardless of everything on this earth that is made to change, the nature of life can not ever be changed. The Spirit of the Creator that made man has a purpose and a way of life planned for him.

DAVID KINDLE: I should like to extend my thanks to the people that made this possible for us of the Indian nations from every part of the country: to come and commune together on the project that we so boldly set forth for us here.

I think of the project here, and back of this project is the love of humanity, the love of man, that men want to improve the lives of their young people in general. The people that sponsored this are to be complimented on the project, and their love of life and desire to live in the way the Great Spirit intended us to live.

ALFRED BOWMAN: It was an inspiration to us that came from Navajo Country to hear this; it all comes back to the origin that was our spiritual life. We should not be ashamed that we recognize a higher being, the Great Spirit that governs all our lives, all the destiny of the universe, as I heard these gentlemen tell when they spoke of the uses of the pipe and of the smoke that doesn't remain at one place but goes out to become universal, just like our informant here says of his corn pollen.

The main objective of all these things is that there must be peace and harmony in the whole universe, and that we must respect our Creator.

E. THOMAS COLOSIMO: In the concluding moments of this project, I would like to express my appreciation to everybody. It isn't an easy project, discussing the philosophy which is the basis for one's life. Many people in this country are friendly to Indians and would like to save Indian culture and to learn from Indians and work with them to make a better society.

Chief Joshua Wetsit wanted me to express his appreciation for participating in the project and his regret at having to leave suddenly this morning before the final session.

ALLEN QUETONE: I don't know whether I can improve on what has been said up to this point in the way of a conclusion, but I want to add some closing remarks here that express my feeling toward the total purpose of the project.

I have always had strong feelings in the direction we have taken, and have always personally looked for some way in which I thought the Indian cultural values could be expressed in the modern world. I think this project is one effort in this direction and this is one reason why I have chosen to take part.

In these difficult times that we are living in, not only for Indian people but for the people of the whole country and of the world, there is a great need to find ways so that people can again have the feeling of human understanding. I think it's the feeling of Mr. Morey and Dr. Winkler that perhaps projects of this kind in some small way can make a contribution toward using the Indian spiritual values and the Indian way of life, as they saw it in nature and in its closeness to the Great Spirit. They found in this feeling of life something that could add to the worth and benefit of all men on earth.

It is difficult in this day to try to express the Indian's place in the modern world. It is very difficult for a young Indian to keep up with the pace that is required if he is to successfully compete in the society and survive. Yet there is a feeling that possibly there may be some spiritual rebirth or renewed understanding of life, so that young Indian people may live in a manner that would be reflective of this natural or spiritual understanding.

I want to thank the sponsors of the project, Dr. Winkler, and Mr. Morey, Mr. Colosimo of Arrow and all the participants in the project.

SYLVESTER MOREY: We believe this is the first time a meeting like this one has been attempted. We appreciate your cordial co-operation in making the discussion so frank and full of life. We hope that many will read the report of the meeting and that some teachers, parents and others will see for themselves how Indian intuitive wisdom can be used to help white men and Indians as well. For years I have read and studied about Indians. So you can imagine what a treat it has been for me to spend a week with you, to come to know you personally, and to listen to your enchanting stories. Thank you.

END

ADDENDA

TO INDIAN YOUTH

I have known Sylvester Morey and Franz Winkler as friends for many years and been closely associated with their work in the Myrin Institute. The inspiring record of this Denver Conference convinces me that the time has at last come when one of their long cherished hopes can actually be realized.

I believe the education of Indian youth can be placed on a new basis, one that will help to set an example also for the better education of white children. This was one of the purposes that from the beginning lay behind the foundation of the Waldorf Institute for Liberal Education at Adelphi University in 1963. The Waldorf Institute, offering the M.A. in education, prepares teachers to recognize, to appreciate, and systematically to develop in their students what Dr. Winkler has called the intuitive faculties, alongside and as a balance for the intellectual. This is being done through the new art of education, the radically new principles and methods that, although inaugurated in Europe fifty years ago by the Austrian philosopher and scientist, Rudolf Steiner, and drawn upon since then by Waldorf schools throughout the world, still belong very much to the future.

Indian youth who are interested in becoming modern teachers, yet in the sense of the Denver conference, may obtain further information by writing the Waldorf Institute for Liberal Education, Adelphi University, Garden City, N. Y. 11530.

John F. Gardner
Adjunct Professor of Education
and Director of the Waldorf
Institute, Adelphi University

115

TO INDIAN ELDERS

The Myrin Institute will welcome further information and opinions from Indian elders on the subject under discussion in this report. The Institute is well aware of the fact that there are many Indians in our country who feel closely connected with the "Indian way of life." These are Indians who still approach life through their heart forces and in whom the creative and intuitive faculties are still very much alive. Now that a first attempt has been made to focus attention on the intuitive side of the American Indian, perhaps enough interest will be shown to warrant further meetings with other groups of Indian elders in the days to come. We hope so.

Sylvester M. Morey, Chairman
The Myrin Institute, Inc.
521 Park Avenue
New York, New York 10021

DATE DUE